SOUL SURVIVORS

SOUL SURVIVORS

Stories of Wounded Women Warriors and the Battles They Fight Long After They've Left the War Zone

KIRSTEN HOLMSTEDT

STACKPOLE BOOKS

Lanham • Boulder • New York • London

Published by Stackpole Books
An imprint of Globe Pequot
Trade Division of The Rowman & Littlefield Publishing Group, Inc.
4501 Forbes Boulevard, Suite 200, Lanham, Maryland 20706
www.rowman.com

Distributed by National Book Network

FIRST EDITION

Library of Congress Cataloging-in-Publication Data

Names: Holmstedt, Kirsten A., author.
Title: Soul survivors : stories of wounded women warriors and the battles
   they fight long after they've left the war zone / Kirsten Holmstedt.
Other titles: Stories of wounded women warriors and the battles they fight
   long after they've left the war zone
Description: Mechanicsburg, PA : Stackpole Books, [2016] | Includes index.
Identifiers: LCCN 2015048240 | ISBN 9780811713795
Subjects: LCSH: Women veterans—United States—Biography. | Women
   soldiers—United States—Biography. | Disabled veterans—United
   States—Biography. | Rape in the military—United States. | Iraq War,
   2003-2011—Women—United States—Biography. | Afghan War,
   2001—Women—United States—Biography.
Classification: LCC U52 .H65 2016 | DDC 362.1092/6970973—dc23 LC record
   available at http://lccn.loc.gov/2015048240

for Lauren Korn, Lisa Pratt,
and all the others in the health care community
who listen to our stories and help us to heal

"There is no honor in suffering."
—a female Marine

Contents

Introduction

MORE WOMEN ARE SERVING IN THE U.S. MILITARY AND SEEING combat than ever before. Since the military's ban on women serving in combat was lifted in 2013, numerous frontline positions have opened up to women, and before that, many women saw combat in Afghanistan and Iraq, where the battlefield did not always follow Pentagon policy. The Department of Veteran Affairs expects female veterans to number more than two million—close to 10 percent of the veteran population—by 2020.

Because more women are serving today, they are at greater risk for the same physical and emotional wounds as the men, including post-traumatic stress disorder (PTSD), traumatic brain injury (TBI), military sexual trauma (MST), suicide, and homelessness. But though men and women confront similar issues after military service, there are differences. For example, PTSD and TBI present themselves differently in women than in men. According to the VA, some PTSD symptoms are more common in women than men. Women are more likely to be jumpy, to have more trouble feeling emotions, and to avoid things that remind them of the trauma than men, who are more likely to feel angry and to have trouble controlling their anger. Women with PTSD are more likely to feel depressed and anxious while men with PTSD are more likely to have problems with alcohol or drugs.

While one in four homeless people is a veteran, the fastest-growing segment of the homeless veteran population appears to be women, many of whom have children. Statistically, female veterans are between two and four times as likely as their civilian counterparts to become homeless, according to recent studies. And if they're young and black, those chances seem to rise. According to Lily Casura, a journalist who was awarded a grant to report on homeless women veterans, "While America might recognize an older, Vietnam-era white male as representative of veteran homelessness, it can miss the new face of veteran homelessness in the shadows—increasingly young, black, female, a recent veteran, often a single mother, with children in tow. Even male veterans are shocked to hear how common a problem precarious housing is for their sister comrades. Because they haven't seen her holding up a cardboard sign at an intersection, panhandling for change or sleeping out in the open, they mistakenly assume—as most of America does—that women veterans aren't going homeless."

Problems such as these show the enormous need for healing after war and military service in general. In this book, I explore the ways our female service members are embracing their trauma and post-traumatic growth and the ways they have committed to their healing. Sometimes the agent of healing is physical, sometimes emotional, sometimes both. There is a mystery to healing. No one knows when or where it will begin or even how long it will take.

Women veterans go to counseling and take medicine to help themselves heal. There's nothing surprising here. In fact, most, if not all, have at least tried counseling and medicine. Those are often, though not always, the first steps in the process toward healing. Some women stay the course with counseling and medicine because it has worked. But many have branched out, often at the suggestion of a counselor, to try different coping skills. Let's face it: when it comes to healing, one size does not fit all. Different approaches work for different people. And more often than not, it takes a variety of activities and people to help someone heal. All the women in this book are warriors who have been challenged physically and emotionally by war or sexual assault, and they have emerged stronger and wiser. They became aware of their challenges and at some point chose to face them head on. These women, against many odds, have chosen to embark on the painful yet rewarding journey of post-traumatic growth.

In order to see the recovery process that has taken place, the reader is first transported back to the early emotional and physical challenges the vets faced. Then you will see the bravery and the resiliency they used to transform and reclaim their lives. For some the road is direct and smooth, but that's seldom the case. "The road to healing is long, hard, messy and incomplete," said Vietnam veteran Linda McClenahan. The book begins with Jen Elliott, a young woman who has just returned from war and has had very little time to address her health needs. As the book progresses, the women have been back for a longer period of time, from conflicts such as Desert Storm and Vietnam; these veterans have the experience of years guiding them.

While this book has to focus on trauma to show the healing that is needed, it's what happens when they return that I want you to focus on. It's what the military and VA did and did not do for them. It's about the resources that are, or must be, available. It's about what the women did for themselves, for ultimately, healing comes from within. The individual must have the will power and desire to heal. Then the community of people and resources can benefit the individual.

My hope is that women who have served will read these stories and find affirmation to help themselves. These remarkable examples of resurrection from the ashes of pain and suffering have much to teach not only women who have served, but men as well. The women in *Soul Survivors*, having emerged from the crucible of trauma with resilience, courage, and compassion, have much to show *all* Americans, who want to help veterans but don't always understand their problems or know how to assist. It's our turn now to learn from them so that others can find their way home.

Trial and Error: The Early Stages of Healing

SPC Jen Elliott

I MET JEN ELLIOTT AT A RESTAURANT IN SACRAMENTO, CALIFORnia. I arrived first. When Elliott walked in, her petite frame, blonde hair, and girlish looks reminded me just how young she was: twenty-two. She was out of the Army now and dressed in civilian clothes. Nothing about her features or clothing screamed soldier, yet I knew Elliott was the warrior I was waiting for because of the tattoo that covered the top half of her chest. Yes, it was that visible. And it had a clear military look to it. Sure enough, the tattoo tells a story, as they so often do with soldiers who endure a war zone: the story of pain and of healing.

But first a little about Elliott. Like many of her fellow soldiers, Elliott comes from a broken family. Her parents split up when she was five. Her mom, who raised her in Rocklin, California, counseled recovering heroin addicts, although with iffy qualifications. Both Elliott's mother and father abused drugs and alcohol, and they exposed Elliott to meth at a young age—she was told it would make cleaning the house less of a chore. When she was

1

fifteen, she started experimenting with cocaine, which became her drug of choice.

Elliott's mom raised Jen and her brother while also earning a master's degree. During those years, Mom passed on her love of education to her daughter. She wanted her children to have a better life than she had. Elliott excelled at school and was selected for a statewide program called GATE (Gifted and Talented Education) in the fourth grade. She graduated when she was sixteen by passing the California High School Proficiency Examination. Graduating early was okay with Elliott, who was a loner and struggled with social anxiety. She started college at seventeen but couldn't afford to stick with it.

That same year, she began dating Mike, who told her of his plan to join the Army. Elliott knew little about the military, but discovered that the Army would pay for her college education, which, for such an avid learner, was an attractive incentive to enlist. After Mike joined the Army, Elliott enlisted. She was seventeen and a half and had postponed her education with plans to return to it in the future—tuition free. She and Mike broke up several months later.

Elliott was excited about the Army because it helped her get off drugs. She never really wanted to do drugs in the first place; they were just familiar to her. Fortunately, the recruiter needed one more person to meet his quota, so he overlooked the fact that she was still using.

In July 2008, Elliott got sober and loved it. She was proud to be a soldier. She deployed to Afghanistan in April 2009 and became a heavy-wheel vehicle operator, driving semi-trucks. Having grown up on a farm, Elliott liked shotguns and considered herself a good shooter, so she also volunteered to be a .50-caliber machine gunner in the rear truck on convoys. As a gunner, her job was to protect the convoy from the enemy.

For the first five months in Afghanistan, Elliott worked every day, without a single weekend off. She was in the respected 32nd Transportation Company from Fort Carson, Colorado. While some companies flipped their trucks because they were top-heavy and driving in mountainous regions, her unit excelled at driving in the mountains and picked up many of the transportation missions over there.

Although she was stationed in Bagram Airfield, Elliott spent most of her time on the road. Her unit did lots of "turns and burns," which meant that if they were on the road for eight hours or less, they would drive to their destination, unload, and then return to their home base. If the mission lasted more than eight hours, they would bed down for a maximum of five hours of sleep. They spent the majority of their time sleeping in tents or on cots. In the summer they put their cots under the truck for shade or tied ponchos together into a canopy. In the winter, when a foot of snow covered the ground, they slept in their trucks and ran the heater.

Her unit was divided into transporters and convoy security. Elliott did security from the rear of the convoy. Several months into the deployment, her convoy got into a firefight. One soldier nearly lost his leg when a rocket-propelled grenade (RPG) went through his truck. It was hard for Elliott to see her friend wounded.

During that same firefight, in which Elliott returned fire, she also had to call for help. This job normally went to another soldier, but that soldier froze and wouldn't call. The medevac, for whatever reason, miscommunication or error, landed in the rear of the convoy while they were still in the kill zone. The medevac was not supposed to land in the kill zone. Elliott was unable to connect with medevac on their radio frequency in the truck, so she had to use her portable radio on top of the vehicle to tell them to get out of the kill zone and land in front of her, where they had front and rear gun support, once they got to the floating rally point. They returned fire and pushed on until they reached the floating rally point about a thousand meters from the firefight. This was the closest area outside the kill zone where the troops felt safe enough to check their ammo and supplies and to assess the wounded. Elliott called her company and told them what was happening. She let the medevac know what color smoke they were going to pop to show where it was safe to land and retrieve the wounded.

"It was the most real feeling in my life," Elliott said. "The sky lit up from the RPG fire, and the debris from the chopper sandblasted my face."

Also riding in the convoys were long-haul jingle trucks, wildly painted Afghan trucks decked out with paintings and with chains attached to the bumper that jingled and chimed as the truck rode over the rough roads. (Supposedly the more chains, the more successful the truck owner and the more he is loved by his wife, a driver told Elliott.) The jingle trucks, commercial vehicles that carry cargoes throughout Afghanistan, often rode in the convoys for safe passage. Sometimes the U.S. military put the jingle trucks in their convoys before and behind trucks carrying super-explosive materials. That way if they were attacked there was a good chance that the Afghan trucks would absorb the blast and be destroyed—and not the Army trucks. Occasionally the plan worked and jingle trucks got blown up.

One day Elliott noticed a jingle truck trying to get into her convoy. Soldiers have rules of engagement, escalating from hand signals to warning shots. She shot at his tire and at his engine. It turned out the driver had been in the convoy, fallen asleep, and then lagged behind the safety of the convoy. He had just been trying to get back in.

Elliott's most memorable day in Afghanistan was September 19, 2009. They had finally moved from living in tents to metal dorms at the airfield in Bagram. Elliott had had a bad day in the motor pool. She had just returned from a mission and wanted to rest, but her sergeant had other plans for her. She had received an award for becoming soldier of the month (think of it as similar to being named employee of the month) and was training to be soldier of the quarter (like soldier of the month, but for a longer and more prestigious three-month period). After being on the road all day and sending the other soldiers on their way, her sergeant made Elliott stay at the motor pool for a couple of hours to work on assembling and disassembling her weapons, which seemed like some form of punishment. When she finally made it back to her barracks, she was exhausted. All she wanted to do was lie down and relax.

At 7:00 in the evening, while most were away, her dorm took a direct hit. Elliott was lying on the top bunk. The last thing she remembers is reading a Nora Roberts book. The explosion knocked her out. When she awoke, it was pitch black. "I thought I was dead," she said. "I couldn't see or hear anything at first."

Her ears were ringing. She doesn't know how long she was lying there on the floor. Maybe a couple of minutes. Then she heard voices. People yelling. She stumbled outside; she did not remember who and where she was until she saw Army uniforms. Her memory returned slowly.

She had been near improvised explosive device (IED) explosions while on past convoys, but this one was different. The sergeant who had made her stay behind and assemble and disassemble her weapon was in the room above her. The explosion killed him. His bed dropped through Elliott's ceiling. Survivor's guilt kicked in almost immediately and continues to trouble her. "I still don't understand it," she said, five years later. "He was married and had children and died. I was eighteen and had nothing going on in my life. I shouldn't have made it." At the very least, she thinks she should have been wounded. She didn't even get hit by shrapnel like the thirteen soldiers outside the barracks who were sent to medical with shrapnel wounds.

After the sergeant was killed and her own near-death experience, Elliott stopped training for soldier of the quarter. The social anxiety that had plagued her in high school returned. She stopped hanging out with other soldiers during the little free time they had; she hid from everyone. She felt God was trying to tell her something by keeping her alive—that maybe she still has a purpose. Otherwise she believes she wouldn't be alive. What made the death of the sergeant even more difficult is that Elliott felt guilty. She had been angry with him at that moment for making her stay behind.

Today a memorial tattoo for her sergeant covers the top half of Elliott's chest. In the center of the tattoo is a grenade, representing a weapon like the one used to kill the sergeant. The valves of a heart are tattooed on the grenade to show that he is now a part of Elliott's heart. Wings on both sides of the grenade represent the sergeant's ascent to heaven. On top of the wings, tattooed skulls symbolized that a part of her had died that day. The skulls have since been replaced with roses. Now she does not want to equate the sergeant's death with a part of her dying, but rather as an experience to learn from. She wants the tattoo to be a memorial, not a reminder of the guilt she felt.

Life in Afghanistan continued to take a turn for the worse after the sergeant's death. Elliott was off the day after the attack. The following day she went back on the road. This wasn't the time to process the death of a comrade. They had a mission. "Charlie Mike," she was told. Continue mission.

But as she continued those missions, she began to have trouble distinguishing between what was real and what was generated by her imagination, by her guilt. She'd see things happening that weren't really happening. Or she would actually see people shooting and blowing things up but wouldn't know if it was real. She wouldn't know if she was supposed to shoot back.

Elliott kept it together as best she could. She was fortunate because when the convoy came under attack, it was usually the front of the convoy shooting back and not Elliott in the rear shooting back. In most attacks she had time to figure out a response, but that dangerous delay in her mind as she tried to determine whether the firefight was real meant possibly fatal danger if the enemy attacked her end of the convoy. Also working in Elliott's favor was the length of the convoy, which stretched out for three miles or more, which gave her time to respond.

In addition to losing her sense of reality, Elliott started to have flashbacks about things she imagined had happened, and migraines from hitting her head against a wall or locker the night her dorm was attacked.

These weakening side effects from the war were tough for Elliott, who took pride in being a soldier. There were few female gunners. She didn't want to ruin it for other women by telling her chain of command that she was often unable to distinguish the actual from what she imagined while on convoys. To avoid that reckoning, she pretended nothing was wrong.

Elliott had been through a lot in her young life—her parents splitting up, their drug use, and subsequently her own drug use—but she had been able to move on. But in Afghanistan, she was having a hard time dealing with firefights and rocket attacks, which she did not understand. And as time passed, as convoys came and went, her doubt grew and fear kicked in, the deadly kind of fear that causes bad things to happen, or lets them happen.

She thinks back to that first day in Afghanistan when she went on a convoy. How fearless she was. She was so new that another soldier had to teach her what to do as a gunner. Yet that's how the craft of being a soldier is really taught—on the job. A soldier gets much preparation for fighting the enemy, but when that time comes, it's critical to have someone on hand who's done it before.

At the time she was an assistant gunner in training, an AG. If a firefight flared, Elliott would hand the gunner the ammo. Sure enough, right away they got into a firefight. She went on autopilot, handing one can of ammo after another to the gunner. She was cool. She was a badass. She wasn't scared because nothing could happen to her; that she knew.

And now? "Now I'm so scared of everything. I fear for my life when I shouldn't or don't need to," she said.

When she joined the Army, Elliott knew she was invincible. "I think that's what makes me struggle now. I thought it would be so fucking cool. I was going to blow shit up. I was wrong."

Odd effects struck. For instance, before the war she was never afraid of heights; now they terrify her. On one mission, she was a driver, or transporter, instead of a gunner, a disruption in her routine that framed another episode.

She had also learned to drive a convoy semi-truck. At some point, regardless of the particular driver or how carefully he or she drives, a convoy truck's tires were going to hang partially off the edge of the rough mountain roads. She told the NCO in the truck that she was afraid of heights and shouldn't drive. She would be fine, he said. She closed her eyes, hit the gas, but dangerously overcompensated. Steering sharply away from the edge, she drove into the mountain. Elliott's panicked maneuver damaged four tires and banged up half the truck. They waited two hours for the truck to be repaired.

Another time her convoy approached a tunnel. As tunnels usually are, these were shaped like an inverted U, so that to clear the tunnel with their high-stacked loads a driver had to steer through the tunnel's very center. Elliott was a passenger in a load truck and had fallen asleep. She was having a nightmare that her truck got blown up by an IED. In that dream-instant, the driver failed to stay dead center. Rolling along at about 45 mph, which is fast for one of these workhorse trucks, the vehicle hit the tunnel with a bone-rattling halt. For a brief, terrifying eternity, it was again a nightmare-come-true experience.

On both occasions, driving into the mountain and then into the tunnel, Elliott was certain she had died. Unaware of where she was, she grew confused and started crying.

She turned to medication. After her dorm was bombed, she could not sleep. She always had slept on her back, but she's been unable to since her sergeant died in the explosion. She was lying on her back when the explosion occurred. In Afghanistan, Elliott sought psychiatric help. Her sleeping problems grew progressively worse, so she began taking Benadryl. That worked for a while, but then she moved on to "benzos," drugs like Valium and Xanax.

Today, Elliott also takes Imitrex for migraines and Ativan for anxiety. She has been told the explosion that threw her off her bed messed up the part of the brain that tells you when to go to sleep. "I can stay up for days if I don't take a sleeping pill. I won't sleep. Anytime I go somewhere overnight, I have to have my sleeping pills."

She sought psychiatric help to get medication but didn't have time for counseling. She was also prescribed Adderall to help her stay awake for long stretches during missions that ran anywhere from twenty-four hours to eighteen days. Imagine the effects of such a combination: drugs to sleep, drugs to keep awake, drugs to calm the nerves, drugs to stop the pain. What could go wrong?

Coming home—first to Fort Carson, Colorado, and then to California—has been an exhausting emotional, mental, and physical roller-coaster ride for Elliott. At first she thought she was fine because soldiers just like her surrounded her. She felt normal until she fell apart. Before she went to war, she was strong emotionally and mentally. Now she was weak. It didn't make sense.

To compensate for this unfamiliar feeling, she bought a semiautomatic rifle that she sleeps with every night still. Elliott was never a drinker but started drinking vodka, first with orange soda and then straight. Then she got into trouble for drinking and fighting. The drinking sent her further out of control, yet she didn't know why, or how to deal with it. She attended anger management classes. She was hospitalized twice, once for attempting suicide and later for being a risk to others. She was a mess.

Today she says she "was mad about everything that happened to me in Afghanistan and I didn't understand. I joined the Army to go to college and be a doctor, and that's not what happened." Before Afghanistan, Elliott thought going into the military was a good idea; it was after 9/11 and her boyfriend, Mike, had joined the Army. Elliott knew there was a chance she would go to war, which was fine with her. She hated her life and was looking for a cause bigger than herself. She wanted to serve her country. Now she gets mad at young adults who want to go to war.

At Fort Carson, Elliott busied herself to keep from having bad thoughts and to stay out of her own head. It was her way of surviving. She enrolled in school online and got her associate's degree in business. After finishing the associate's degree, she started a bachelor's degree in psychology. She needed to keep very busy, to distract herself from creeping darkness. When she wasn't working, studying, or playing racquetball, she was taking care of cats and dogs at a shelter in Colorado Springs. She couldn't have an animal of her own because she lived in the barracks; the shelter was the next best thing. Every day Elliott did the same thing. The routine was one she could live by, even though she was still drinking at the time.

In 2012, after one year in Afghanistan, Elliott left the Army after four years and returned to California. Although she had considered staying in the Army and even put in orders to go to Fort Drum, New York, when she learned that the unit was deploying to Afghanistan, she freaked out and decided instead to finish her enlistment and get out of the Army. It wasn't until she moved away from the other soldiers that she realized how much help she needed. "I had no idea how much my stuff was bothering me," she said. "No one really talked about it." She and the other soldiers had built an unspoken support system. They knew what each other was going through and supported one another, almost by osmosis. In California, Elliott didn't know any soldiers. Instead, civilians who often made inappropriate comments surrounded her. "Did you kill anyone?" "It must have been so cool being a gunner." "Being in explosions must have been awesome."

Then the panic attacks started, one of which caused a seizure. She still experiences flashbacks. When they occur they last for hours and Elliott doesn't know where she is.

One day in California, Elliott saw a dead dog on a railroad track. In that microscopic instant she was back in war. "That's what we saw in Afghanistan," she said. Dogs were stuffed with bombs and left on the side of the road. "It was very fucked up."

After seeing the dog, Elliott went home to get her cell phone; she wanted to take a picture of the dog on the track. She had a message on her phone. It was an automatic Facebook message asking her to celebrate the birthday of a friend who had been killed in Afghanistan. She broke down. Then came New Year's Eve and fireworks. She just wanted to crawl under her bed—with her gun. Elliott didn't know how to deal with it all.

Help came in many forms, including her dog, detox, group and private therapy, and Narcotics Anonymous/Alcoholics Anonymous meetings. She credits her German shepherd/wolf named Timber with saving her life. "I wouldn't be here if it weren't for Timber," she said. When Elliott gets upset, Timber lies down with his head on the back of her neck. When she has nightmares, he jumps on her back, wakes her, and stays with her until she has calmed down. "Everything that I do and plan is about my dog," Elliott said. "My dog is my Prozac. He gave me something to care for because I didn't think I had anything when I came back. I didn't think I had anything to offer. I had a degree and had been in the Army but had no hope, no joy, no positive outlook on life. I just didn't care anymore."

Elliott continued drinking a lot and when she couldn't quit on her own ended up in detox. She had become so antisocial that she could not connect with anyone. She wasn't using the VA as a resource. She tried to kill herself again. She has a history of overdosing on pills when she doesn't know what to do, and she did not know what to do when she got out of the Army.

After she went through detox and got out of recovery, Elliott decided she could do this. She could heal and cope with her mental health challenges, her post-traumatic stress disorder (PTSD), and her traumatic brain injury.

She began to work hard at her recovery. There were times when she attended group therapy three to four times a week, including a women's group, cognitive behavioral therapy (CBT), and Seeking Safety therapy. The women's group was led by Katie Grace Bell. Elliott, who's been around enough counselors to know, describes Bell as the best she's come across. "She has been the most influential person in my life," Elliott said. "I wouldn't be sober if it weren't for Katie. She got me into detox and then transitional living. I couldn't stay in a place by myself because I wanted to get high. Katie has a huge heart and will help anybody."

In 2013, while in transitional housing, Elliott met Barrett Rupp. He became her boyfriend and helped her talk about her PTSD. He was one of the first people she opened up to. They got sober and moved in together.

Elliott began volunteering at the VA; she finished her bachelor's degree. Her goal when she came back from Afghanistan was to continue schooling because she loved to learn. She chose psychology, thinking she could learn about herself. Elliott loves psychology, but now she doesn't want to be a psychologist. She made a realistic appraisal of her life and believes her problems will never go away. Elliott needs to learn how to cope with her issues, which she feels is the best she can hope for. "I go to someone for therapy because I want to talk to someone who knows their shit and can give me advice because I have no idea," she said. "I don't want to go to some person who knows nothing about it and is so fucked up that that's why they decided to become a psychologist. That would have been me."

Elliott's goal is to give back by working with veterans who suffer from PTSD and substance problems. The process is effective, she said. In just three months of working with the vets, she could tell she had come a long way. "I'm still not healed. I don't think I'll ever be healed. I know that," Elliott said. But if she keeps adding to her toolbox of coping skills, when a stressful situation occurs she is prepared and not taken off guard.

For Elliott, healing is about having serenity in her life. "I've felt moments of serenity. They come and go. Things get really good and I feel it and start doing a lot." That's often followed by feeling overwhelmed, when she has to take a step back and regroup. That's the cycle. The key for Elliott is to keep herself from obsessing and to maintain a positive attitude. "I do have a lot of hope today and I know things are going to get better," she said. She is better able to put things in perspective. These sound like clichés, but Elliott realizes that change will not happen overnight or on its own.

"I've always been cut off from the world because of my anxiety and never really interacted with people," she said. Elliott's never had many friends, which means she hasn't had people close enough to her to point out what was wrong or how she had changed. Elliott lived and suffered in a bubble that she never realized she had created for herself. She never talked to other people about what was going on in her life, and so never heard from them that they experience their own problems. Without that personal feedback, Elliott thought she and her problems were special, unique, one of a kind.

She now understands that many people share her problems. She's not so unique and messed up after all. "Some of the things that I think are so wrong with me I realize are normal by talking to people," Elliott said. "It's just that other people don't overanalyze like I do. . . . I'm learning that I'm an introvert and that doesn't mean I'm fucked up," she added. "It's just a personality trait."

Elliott never cared what other people thought about her; now she does. The more she talks to others, the more she realizes their intentions are not to hurt her. So she talks to people more, works on her life, and makes a little progress each day. She finds it helps to put herself in situations where she is vulnerable.

Talking to people and putting things in perspective is really important. And practicing not getting down on herself. Her boyfriend, Barrett, helps by pointing out when she is being hard on herself.

She still goes to NA and AA meetings. They keep her centered and around people who suffer from the same problems she has, whom she understands and who understand her. When she drinks and does drugs, it's to make everything in her head go away. It's a way of not dealing with her stuff.

She's trying not to run away from her problems. She has developed faith in her health care providers and their opinions. They tell her that she will get better, but that it may not look the way she imagined. They tell her it will take time. The meetings get her around other people who don't judge her. There is always someone in the room with more problems.

Elliott feels comfortable talking about her Army days. If it weren't for those meetings, she wouldn't be sharing her story with us, with you and me. The meetings have helped her talk to people. One of the major symptoms of PTSD is avoidance. The meetings have encouraged her to stop avoiding people.

She's reaching out for help and taking the advice of others. "I tried for years to maintain my life and I've been miserable," Elliott said. "I'm getting better . . . much better. I'm not where I was a year ago when I got out of the Army. I was in a very, very bad place. The past year has been very healing." She's learning how to take care of herself on her own. She never did that before. She's learning how to talk to people, open up, feel vulnerable, love. Her relationships used to be like a truck and a trailer. When she felt pain, Elliott would disconnect the trailer and drive away. She was fine with that. She's not like that anymore. Now she allows herself to feel the pain of relationships.

Being open to trying new activities is important to her. It's helping her find her niche. Healing is unique to each individual. "Some do yoga," Elliott said. "I can't. If I did just that or just group therapy, it wouldn't help. I'm finding as many different things as I can—positive stuff—to stay busy. . . . It's easy for me to avoid the world. I know how to do it well. I could make it where no one knows that I exist. I did that for a long time. Now I just want to be happy, and I have hope. That's the only thing that's getting me through, because I never had hope [before]," she said.

Still, she has many fears. With the way she thinks and understands the world, she wonders if she will ever be like other people, at least in the way she feels other people think and understand. "I know I get closer to it every day when I try. But if I sit at home and feel sorry for myself, I don't make any progress."

"It's nice to know you're not alone," she said. "I'm not alone. I'm not alone. I'm not alone."

Since our first interview, Elliott, Barrett, and Timber moved from California to Virginia. A nonprofit agency, Military Warriors Support Foundation/Homes for Heroes, gave her a repossessed house that has been renovated. Elliott is working full-time and feeling great about her life.

Ain't No Mountain High Enough

Lt. Col. Kathy Champion

KATHY CHAMPION WAS NINE YEARS OLD WHEN SHE WENT TO A parade and saw soldiers in uniform. Seeing them made her feel so proud that she told her grandparents that, like the soldiers, someday she was going to defend her country.

Then came the West Point debate: Should women even be allowed to attend? "I remember watching the news and thinking, 'Why can't I go to West Point?'" That was 1976, the first year women were allowed to enroll—and 119 of them did. Four years later, sixty-two women graduated from West Point. Kathy wasn't one of them, but her childhood commitment had been serious and nine years later she fulfilled that promise, making a career of the Army, serving first in the reserves and then on active duty for nearly three decades.

Champion joined the Army reserves in 1982 to become a combat medic/paramedic. She was seventeen. She was happy going to the monthly drills and summer training while she pursued her civilian career as a science teacher for middle school

17

through college students. To Kathy Champion, military training was a break from her daily life. It gave her the best of both worlds. Meanwhile, she became a mom and began raising a son and a daughter. As a reservist, Champion said she was like any other mom. She taught during the day and went to ball games after work. When she had reserve duty, her spouse watched the children. Her daughter was a good student. School came easy to her and she was involved in a lot of activities. Her son was a social butterfly who did what he had to in order to stay in sports.

While in the reserves, Champion served in Bosnia with U.S. peacekeeping forces (1996–97). Her children stayed with her spouse when she deployed. By now she was a captain, and one day she ran into her brother, also a soldier, in Sarajevo. It was a pleasant surprise. Champion also went on active duty from 2001 to 2007 when she was a civil affairs officer, training with troops for Middle East missions. She traveled to Saudi Arabia, Qatar, and Kuwait, where she and other commanders prepped for battle.

She served in Afghanistan in 2003–4. In 2005–6 she deployed to Iraq, where she became a lieutenant colonel commanding the Alpha Company of the 448th Civil Affairs Battalion from Fort Lewis, Washington. There she led a unit of thirty-two men, some of whom did not make it home. The civil affairs unit was responsible for the zoo, schools, hospitals, and city councils in the small towns that made up western and southern Baghdad. She was the liaison between the military and the local mayors/governor. Champion was charged with rehabilitating the community. She worked with the 1st Brigade of the 10th Mountain Division and the 256th Louisiana National Guard Brigade. The commanders made their wish list, and her unit set out to make it happen for and with them.

Her background as a medic enabled her to evaluate the health needs of the Iraqis and treat them for cuts, inoculate them, and provide them with antibiotics for colds and flu. She was able to deliver babies and help save Iraqi soldiers wounded in combat. One time she set up triage in a village to provide medical care for the locals. So many Iraqis turned out that they had to erect a wire fence to control the heavy flow of people. Included in the unfortunate mass was a little girl dressed in yellow and wearing sandals. Her face was dirty and her hair looked like it hadn't been washed in months. The girl was so determined to see Champion that she climbed through the wire fence. As she squeezed through, she cut herself above her amber eyes. Champion cleaned the injury and stitched it up while the girl thanked her profusely in Arabic. The girl had a fierceness in her eyes that matched her actions. It turned out that she hadn't come for herself. The child's mother was pregnant, and the little girl wanted Champion to go with her to see her pregnant mother and to make sure she was all right.

The girl's mother wouldn't go to the Americans, so the young girl had gone to them instead. When the child looked into Champion's eyes, the lieutenant colonel crumbled. Champion gave in, even though she wasn't supposed to leave the safety of the wire. The mother lived about a quarter mile away. After looking her over, Champion determined that the mother's health was in no danger.

The experience with the young girl was a far cry from what had happened earlier in the day. The clinic Champion had been evaluating was attacked by soldiers who had begun firing on the Iraqi people visiting the clinic. Now Champion was trying to save civilian lives. This was a conundrum she still wrestles with on a regular basis. One of Champion's biggest challenges then and now is coming to terms with the fact that one minute she was saving Iraqis and the next she was being attacked by them.

On another day she treated two Iraqi boys for infections and then went to a council meeting. As she left the meeting and headed toward her Humvee, the vehicle exploded. Soldiers caught the boys who had used remote control devices to cause the explosion. As Champion sat in a daze on the curb, she wondered: Was it worth the effort to help these people?

When a new commander arrived to take over her job, Champion took him out to show him what a typical day was like. First they went to a two-room medical clinic (hut) that not only had to be staffed but also maintained. Meanwhile, they took sniper fire. They killed the sniper and moved on to their next location, a council meeting at a different village down the road. While they were talking to tribal members in the meeting, they were ambushed by a group of men in masks with AK-47s (rifles). A quick-reaction force helped get them out of the building.

After that they drove to a school. On their way, having just turned off the freeway, the new commander's vehicle hit an IED. An already-long day just got longer as they had to sit and wait for a tow truck to take away the disabled vehicle. They met with the headmaster at the elementary school and ended their day by handing out candy and Beanie Babies to the Iraqi children.

Over the course of her deployment, the various Humvees that Champion traveled in hit seven different IEDs on the roads outside Baghdad. Two were direct hits, and the other five were within 50–100 feet. Twice she was wounded. Then, in July 2005, her arm was wounded on the battlefield. She flew back to the United States, recovered, and returned to Iraq on her birthday, September 26, to continue her tour as a civil affairs company commander.

When she finally came home in August 2006, Champion was physically broken yet believed she was still all right emotionally. It took her five years to fully regain the use of her arm. She was wounded in her left leg, and another explosion blew out her left eardrum. In addition, accumulating back injuries and headaches added to the total effect of serious bodily impairment, which she bore like a soldier.

All these injuries were from IEDs detonating near trucks in which she rode or drove. There were plenty of days in Iraq when her wounds made her want to give up, but she wasn't one to let the enemy win. There were even days when she thought the enemy would win.

Emotionally, Champion thought she could leave the war behind now that she was back home. That didn't happen. In Iraq she saw too much and endured too many horrors to act as if nothing had happened. For instance, one of her female Iraqi interpreters was kidnapped and murdered, and her head shipped to her parents. The killers left the body for the troops to find. The dead woman's parents blamed Champion. The parents knew the U.S. troops got their daughter involved in the war and that they had promised to protect her. "This is because of you," they said to Champion. There was nothing Champion could say. "The daughter sacrificed herself for the cause," she said years later.

She remembered the day they uncovered an unrefrigerated morgue. It was full of bodies that were to be buried without a proper burial. The bodies were stacked like flattened cardboard boxes. The stench was so dreadful that it haunts Champion still. "I smell that smell and it puts me back there to that day and opening the door of the morgue," she said. The smell reminds her of the pictures of liberated concentration camps during World War II and the varying degrees of carnage the liberators found.

In addition to what already ailed her, Champion began to lose vision in one eye. The blindness occurred on October 3, 2008, two years after returning from Iraq. Other than her shoulder and leg injuries, she had thought she was relatively healthy. She had been able to exercise again and participate in running events. Then came that October morning. Her left eye went blank, sightless. She had had a severe migraine that she thought was causing her loss of vision.

But the sight in the left eye never came back. In May 2009, her right eye began to deteriorate. Now she has no sight in her left eye and sees only light and dark shadows through her right eye. A neurologist gave her a year to live, though that death sentence eventually was retracted.

She has been treated for Devic's Syndrome, a disease that inflames and damages the optic nerve and spinal cord, at the Mayo Clinic and at the Walter Reed National Military Medical Center in Washington, D.C. The Mayo Clinic concluded she did not have Devic's but that she definitely had contracted some type of damaging virus while providing medical care in Iraq, one that attacks the optical nerve. Champion is one of about 8,000 soldiers affected by this nervous and autoimmune system disease that mainly attacks women, zaps them of their energy, and can affect their sight and nervous systems. In Champion's case, the virus temporarily inflamed her entire spinal cord, preventing her from moving the left side of her body or even walking.

Soon after she lost her vision, Champion received notification that she was on the promotion list to be a colonel, with a possible assignment to the Pentagon. This was in line with her goal of becoming a general. But she turned down the promotion. She didn't want to be a pitiable blind person working at the Pentagon. "I couldn't be the soldier I wanted to be," she said. "I didn't want to be known as a blind colonel." Turning down the promotion was a hard decision. The Army had been her life, her identity, and a great source of pride. "It was who I identified myself with," she said. "Not a teacher, but a soldier."

Instead of a promotion, Champion chose a medical discharge from active duty in the Army for PTSD, traumatic brain injury, blindness, and other injuries. She went from active duty back to reserve duty until August 18, 2009. She would have to remake herself physically and emotionally.

During reserve duty, Champion again taught science for middle school and high school students and at a college in Washington State. Yet, although she had a degree in education, it began to sink in that she no longer wanted to teach. Her PTSD prevented her from being around a lot of people. She applied for a doctoral program in marine science at the University of South Florida. She started college and was having fun. But as her eyesight further deteriorated, a job she got doing research ended. She could no longer see well enough to do her job.

Champion finally left the reserves when she became too sick to work. Once she left the Army, she began to run out of money. Soon she was kicked out of her apartment. She went from doing well financially to living out of her car, sitting on park benches and watching the ducks. "I was so mortified I couldn't take care of myself," she said. At the time she didn't enroll in the VA to receive benefits because she didn't think she qualified.

In 2010, just before Christmas, Champion hit rock bottom. Her response was to swallow a lot of pills and drink wine until she overdosed. She was feeling very alone at the time and didn't want to live. She didn't have the Army.

She has family, but was too proud to tell them about her problems or to ask for help. Her son and daughter are now in their twenties. No one knew. "I was too ashamed to ask for help," Champion said. "I didn't want my children to know their mother had failed and wasn't able to take care of herself, when all their lives I was the rock in the family." Her family turned to her when they needed help emotionally, physically, and financially. "I was the one who provided the support," she said. "I was the strong one. When I couldn't be the rock, it was horrifying."

Sometimes it is easier to accept help from a stranger than from a family member. In 2007–8, Champion caught a lucky break when an acquaintance introduced her to Beverly Young, the wife of Congressman Bill Young. The friend told Beverly that she had to help Champion, a decorated veteran. Congressman Young helped her with all her VA and social security benefits. Beverly gave Champion money and told her to use it to get off the park bench and find a home. Champion rented an apartment, made her car payments, bought food and clothes, and stretched out the money until she got help from the VA.

The healing had begun. "Through the graciousness of one person I was able to get back on my feet again," she said.

To help her cope with her blindness, Champion got a guide dog named Angel on April 1, 2009. Angel, part golden retriever, part Labrador, helped Champion deal with her PTSD. Angel took her outdoors, where she is most comfortable. When growing up, Champion had taken her brothers camping, fishing, and hunting. She's always liked sailing and going to the ocean. The first chance she got, Champion took Angel hiking into the Grand Canyon. She trusted Angel 100 percent. Angel gave her back her active life.

Champion has since assembled a visual documentary of where the two have been to show others that, despite once being around "dangerous and evil people" in a war zone, now she was doing well again. She and Angel went to space camp together, climbed in Colorado, and dived with whale sharks at the Georgia Aquarium. And wherever they traveled in the United States, they took time to help wounded warriors.

Then in 2012, during a summer workshop for veterans with PTSD, Champion and Angel were attacked by another dog that caught them from behind. After that, Angel could no longer focus on guiding Champion. Attempts to retrain Angel didn't work, and she was retired in December 2012 to live out her days with her puppy raisers in North Carolina.

Champion got a new dog, George, an 85-pound pure black Labrador from Southeastern Guide Dogs, Inc. They have gone hiking in Colorado and North Carolina, and Champion hopes to hike the Grand Canyon from rim to rim. Also a triathlete, Champion can count on George meeting her at the 500-meter mark and finishing the race with her.

It took a few years, but in April 2013 Champion began to seriously focus on herself. That's when she knew she wanted to stay alive and fight for herself. But to do that she would need emotional, physical, and mental help. She sought counseling and medical care to get off her medications. She completed her first Olympic triathlon: a 1.5-kilometer (.93-mile) swim, 40-kilometer (25-mile) bike, and 10-kilometer (6.2-mile) run.

Now, Champion says she likes who she is. "I'm a free spirit. . . . I enjoy experiencing things instead of being scared to death and hiding in my house." She lives in a small house by the beach in Gulfport, Florida, and enjoys life.

Experiencing new things keeps life interesting and makes it challenging in a good way. She wasn't going to let her war wounds hold her back. The athletic side of Champion took over and moved her forward. She did a five-day, 400-mile bike ride from New Orleans to Tallahassee with civilians and other veterans. She rode on the back of a tandem bike with a pilot at the controls.

Champion struck gold when she learned about Soldiers to Summits (S2S), a nonprofit organization. According to the S2S website, the group "empowers veterans to overcome barriers and reclaim lives. In this program, mountains serve as both metaphor and training ground for wounded soldiers as they stretch goals, build world-class teams, innovate through adversity and step up to lead and serve others. Integrated with the rehab process, S2S helps soldiers restructure how they approach their past and future."

On June 1, 2013, Champion went on her first climb with other veterans and civilians. She climbed Mount Bierstadt in Colorado, more than 14,000 feet. She had recently finished a triathlon, so she thought she was in good-enough shape, and although the altitude proved to be a challenge, it wasn't anything she couldn't handle. Like in the heat of the Iraqi desert, Champion was able to acclimate herself.

This was the first time Champion would climb as a blind woman. She didn't know how to act or how to be surefooted so they gave her a guide. For many people the payoff for hiking a mountain is the view along the way and from the top. She couldn't see the view, so her guide described it to her.

"It was exhilarating," said Champion, who learned on that hike that she had more strength than she thought. She was reminded of when she was in college; she would draw pictures of mountains and draw points on them that represented her goals.

"When I do these outdoor sports, I feel like there are no limits to my experience in life," Champion said. "Outdoor sports are made up of a lot of small steps, and life is the same way. You have to take life one step at a time. And when you reach the summit or the end of the trail, that's what gives you a sense of hope. For me, being outside is freeing. It's about me showing others how to take small steps. Even if I fall along the trail, I will still get up and move forward."

After that hike in Colorado, Champion applied and was accepted to climb in Peru on October 2, 2013. She and twelve other wounded warriors went to Peru, but first they trained in Telluride, Colorado. Following the training, the hikers met in Miami to fly together to Peru. During their first week there, they stayed in the mountains with descendants of the Inca. They helped to build an elementary school kitchen, a guinea pig pen, and solar panels to improve the lives of the Incas. Native high school students spent time with them in ceremonial activities. These students had never seen blind people and amputees before seeing Champion and the other wounded warriors. They were educating each other.

They were at 15,000 feet for five days when Champion got altitude sickness. Her lungs filled with water and she felt like she was suffocating. She went down to 11,500 feet but still couldn't get the water out of her lungs, so she returned to Cuzco and was taken by emergency evacuation to Lima. At this point, she was no longer with any of the people from Soldiers to Summits. She was on her own. She is proud of her inner strength and her ability to communicate in Spanish with her doctors and nurses. She returned to the States, where she was hospitalized for two days.

After her release, she went to the grocery store with a friend. Champion was craving juice. Usually when she grocery shops she keeps a scented dryer sheet near her face when approaching the butcher department so that she smells the dryer scent and not the raw meat. Otherwise she has flashbacks. She had flashbacks on this particular day. One of Champion's duties in Iraq was to oversee a zoo and make sure the animals were fed. She recalled watching the zookeepers butcher donkeys and feed them to the lions. She'd watch the lions tear up the meat. Then she'd remember Iraqi body parts strewn about after a firefight or explosion.

Despite all the lingering issues, Champion is building a foundation, True North Champions. She considers this her job, although she doesn't have to work because she gets retirement from the military, as well as 100 percent disability from the military and VA. Nonetheless, Champion is growing the foundation to include a wellness center so that veterans of all generations can come and heal and take a break.

The purpose of the foundation is to meet veterans where they are in their lives. It's all anonymous. Champion thrives on helping women get beyond thoughts of worthlessness and lets them know that, like her, they will find a way. That there is hope. "I just help them and ask them to pay it forward when they get on their feet," she said. "I try to be a Beverly Young now," she said, referring to the Florida woman who helped lift her up when she'd been really down.

One day she got a call from a soldier at Walter Reed. His dad was in the hospital in Florida. Could she see if he was OK? Champion sent a chaplain to look in on the dad, who later was moved from the hospital to the VA hospital. She was able to get the family from Walter Reed down to Florida and provide a home for them as well as a job for the soldier. Wells Fargo and Bank of America donated a foreclosed house, mortgage free, to the wounded warrior.

In 2014, Champion started trying different sports—rowing in Oklahoma City; cycling in Colorado Springs at the Olympic Training Center; kayaking on a river in Charlotte, North Carolina; and sailing in Sonar boats, created for use by the disabled, with other disabled athletes. This led to Champion competing for a southeast regional triathlon championship. Champion won the regional championship for her division. She went on to compete in the National Para-cycling Championships and took fourth place. Now she is trying to qualify for the Paralympic Cycling Team. She will know in April 2016 if she made the team. Champion was also in charge of a weeklong hike in Colorado for herself and three other blind women.

Champion has partnered with others to find PTSD dogs and therapy dogs for veterans. She works with Sirius K9, Vets Helping Heroes, K9s for Warriors, and Paws for Patriots. All of these organizations help veterans receive service dogs. Champion still relies on her guide dog for emotional support and believes talking to George helps her through the nights of bad dreams and stressful events.

She may be retired from the military, but Champion says she will continue to help fellow veterans. And in doing so she helps herself. "It keeps me out of the dark hole," she said. "I don't feel useless. I may not be doing what I used to do, but I feel successful again internally."

How far has she come?

People ask her, "How can you be so positive? You're blind."

"I don't see it as a negative," she said.

Give 'em Hell
Sgt. Tegan Griffith

IT WASN'T UNTIL APRIL 2013 THAT TEGAN GRIFFITH REALIZED she had a voice and could put it to use as an advocate for veterans.

During the eulogy at her grandfather's funeral, Griffith's dad, Glen, talked about the traits of each of the grandchildren that he thought they had inherited from his dad. When he got to Tegan, he referred to her as a little person who had been given a big voice. But Griffith, an Iraq war veteran, didn't always have a big voice. Actually, she says she was empowered by her dad's words that April morning.

The last time she talked to her grandfather was the night before she went to the White House with the advocacy group Iraq and Afghanistan Veterans of America (IAVA). As her grandmother was repeating the phone conversation to her grandfather, he shouted in the background, "Give 'em hell!" It became her life motto.

Griffith traveled to Capitol Hill that week with IAVA, which had chosen her and others to participate in the premiere of the advocacy and leadership development program Storm the Hill. She was armed with information. Griffith brought her personal story—the pride of being a Marine during wartime. The "Stormers," as the group called itself, brought attention to many issues, including the backlog of benefits at the VA, military sexual trauma (MST), the high suicide rate among vets, and the 30,000 vets who were forcibly discharged based on a personality disorder instead of the more likely diagnosis of post-traumatic stress or traumatic brain injury.

Griffith was assigned to Team Bravo for IAVA's Storm the Hill. Team Bravo went to her state representative's office. Mark Pocan, representing Wisconsin's 2nd Congressional District, wasn't there that day, but Griffith passed along her group's message to his legislative assistant.

The following year, Griffith and three other members of IAVA formed Team Delta. The group returned to Representative Pocan's office, and this time the congressman was there. They talked for a few minutes about a computer software company that could help make health care records seamless between the Department of Defense (DoD) and the U.S. Department of Veterans Affairs. Pocan told her that whatever she needed, he had her back. He referred her to his office and to some constituents in Madison, Wisconsin. Since forming that relationship with Pocan's office, Griffith has been invited to listening sessions, where veterans talk and politicians listen. She said it was cool to meet with her representative in the nation's capital and then again back in her hometown. Pocan was just one of many representatives and senators Griffith met that day in D.C. From morning until evening, the IAVA teams met with representatives from nearly every state.

In July 2014, Griffith flew to D.C. with IAVA to support the parents of deceased Marine Clay Hunt, who had been a corporal and member of IAVA and who died by suicide in 2011. For three hours, his parents offered their thoughts on veterans' access to mental health care before the House Committee on Veterans' Affairs. The Clay Hunt Suicide Prevention for American Veterans Act (now called the SAV Act) was introduced on July 10, 2014, by Congressman Tim Walz (D-MN1) and by House Committee on Veterans' Affairs chairman Congressman Jeff Miller (R-FL1). The bill passed the House on December 9 of that year.

The Senate version of the SAV Act (S.2930) was introduced on November 17, 2014, by Senators John McCain (R-AZ), Richard Blumenthal (D-CT), Richard Burr (R-NC), Roy Blount (R-MO), Lisa Murkowski (R-AK), and Joe Manchin (D-WV). The bill failed in the Senate after Sen. Tom Coburn (R-OK) placed a hold on the legislation, preventing it from being considered before the Senate adjourned for the year. When the 114th session of Congress began in January 2015, IAVA refocused its efforts and reintroduced the bill. President Obama signed the act February 12, 2015. Griffith and several other veterans were brought to Washington, D.C., to witness the signing.

The Clay Hunt Suicide Prevention for American Veterans Act will help the Department of Veterans Affairs study new strategies for suicide prevention and give student loan incentives to recruit psychiatrists who agree to work with veterans.

Before she even thought of becoming an advocate, Griffith was a Marine. She joined the Corps in July 2005. She tried college first, but then got caught up in the adventure and wanderlust of the Marine Corps. Her brother preceded her in the Corps and then joined the National Guard in North Carolina when his enlistment was over. Joining the Marine Corps was Griffith's way of ribbing her brother. "If he can do it, so can I," she said.

Upon reaching the Fleet Marine Corps, Griffith was stationed at Camp Pendleton. Griffith deployed to Al-Taqaddum (known to all U.S. military as TQ) Air Base in Iraq with an attack helicopter squadron from April to November 2008, where she worked in quality assurance as a program manager for the technical publications library. She was a central source of information for her squadron, the UH-1N (a medium military helicopter) and the AH-1W (a twin-engine attack helicopter), and their crews and maintainers. If a change came out, such as a vehicle recall, she would be the trained individual to notify squadron personnel. While deployed, she was responsible for obtaining, auditing, and cataloging the most current information for the squadron.

In TQ, Griffith had a "sexual encounter" with a drunk Marine. And as is often the case, the lack of action that followed from her immediate chain of command left her frustrated. She immediately reported the incident to her sergeant, who was also drunk. He had been drinking with her perpetrator. Her staff sergeant also had been drinking with them and failed to report the incident. Griffith finally approached a respected gunnery sergeant in another shop. "He did the right thing and took it up the chain," she said. "He listened to me."

The sexual assault report brought in two uniformed victim advocates, one male and one female, both officers. The female was sent to another forward operating base (FOB) shortly after the incident, so Griffith couldn't talk to her. She sought out the combat stress unit on TQ for several sessions. She e-mailed her father, Glen Griffith, about the incident. He is career Army and was an Equal Opportunity representative for his unit. He forwarded her e-mail to Headquarters Marine Corps, who then contacted her commanding officer in Iraq. The next day she was escorted by her officer in charge to the commanding officer's office to explain the incident. There was a public non-judicial punishment (NJP) held by the command, and the perpetrator got a thirty-day restriction.

Griffith didn't feel as though she was in any danger in Iraq—from the enemy. But then, define "enemy."

Once she returned to San Diego, it was hard for Griffith to continue in her squadron. She felt alienated from the Marines in her shop. The good old boy network didn't have any room for a female corporal. Her discomfort in the squadron was challenging and escalated quickly. It was during this time that Griffith decided not to reenlist in the Marine Corps and received orders back to her original unit to finish her contract. She again became the program manager for a large technical publications library, where she trained new Marines checking in and became an asset to the 3rd Marine Aircraft Wing inspection team. She received a Navy and Marine Corps Achievement Medal for the program, passing the most significant audit the Department of the Navy holds, the Commander Naval Air Forces (CNAF) audit, with few discrepancies.

Griffith noticed that the Marine Corps had changed in one way for the better and for the worse in another. Despite the sexual harassment, she loved being a Marine. "I wouldn't be who I am today without the Marine Corps," she said.

It has given her a better understanding of who she is as a person. She describes herself as having been ignorant prior to the deployment. She came home an adult. She doesn't sweat the small stuff and realizes the importance of maintaining relationships with family and friends to help keep her grounded.

She isn't as naïve as her pre-deployment self. She went to war "bright-eyed and bushy-tailed." Today she is more mature and cautious. When she sees a photo of herself in uniform in Iraq, she doesn't recognize herself. For the most part, she lived in the comfort and safety of TQ, which had been built up considerably before she arrived. It had a Green Beans coffee shop, shuttle buses, and an air-conditioned chow hall on base. She felt guilty about these amenities because she knew fellow Marines who had it worse than she did.

Griffith became fragile emotionally after her tour in Iraq. She developed a temper and was intolerant of men in authority roles. This made it hard for her to keep a steady job. In hindsight, she realizes she was dealing with the sexual incident in Iraq and the lack of leadership that followed. At the time, the women in that unit seemed to be treated as distractions instead of peers. She remembers a time on deployment when her gunnery sergeant said that several men were distracted by the women's breasts when they were "half-mast"—where coveralls are rolled down and fastened at the waist, or when wearing just utility trousers and a T-shirt without a blouse. She was ordered to counseling for talking back after his comment to her.

In 2009, Griffith got out of the Marine Corps, but it took her another four years to get a full-time job. She struggled to find meaningful employment, partly because she was trying to deal with her own issues of leaving the Marine Corps. "I didn't know how to manage my anger or frustrations," Griffith said. "I also had no idea what I wanted to be now that I wasn't an active-duty Marine." She hadn't planned to leave the Marine Corps after only one enlistment until she actually deployed. After her harassment, she decided she didn't like the direction of the Corps. Leaving it was the most difficult decision she's made.

While Griffith was transitioning out of the Corps, she didn't get much help from the transition class taught for separating Marines. The only thing Griffith has left from her class in 2009 is a name tag and a subscription to Corporate Gray (an organization that helps vets find jobs after the military) e-mails that have arrived consistently since 2009. In February 2014, she was able to meet with a newly retired base sergeant major on Camp Pendleton who is now responsible for leading the Transition GPS program there. Griffith learned about the different tracks Marines can choose, such as education or entrepreneurship.

Today, separating servicemembers receive a more personalized approach for their transition versus the old one-size-fits-all class. "I feel I would have definitely benefited from a personalized track when I left the Marine Corps," Griffith said. "When the instructor went around the classroom asking each Marine what our plans were, I told him, 'I'm going to use the money I saved on deployment and take a cross-country road trip.'" In hindsight, Griffith knows that wasn't a realistic approach. "We all just wanted to be out of there," she said.

The problem with programs for transitioning servicemembers is that they are often developed by individuals who are still in the military and who have never experienced transition. That's another reason Griffith actively participated in advocacy work with IAVA. The more post–9/11 veterans who become advocates and speak on behalf of their demographic, the better the programs will be for them.

While unemployed, Griffith sold her car to avoid losing it in small-claims court. Her credit score plummeted. She moved eight times in those four years and had run out of options. She didn't have a steady full-time job and relied on her disability compensation from the VA. She attributes her lack of meaningful employment in part to "the big ego the military gives you when you get out, especially in the Marine Corps," Griffith said. "They tell you the world is veteran-friendly, and that employers will roll out the red carpet and hire you because you're a veteran. An education would essentially fall into your lap with little or no effort." She learned a lot of things the hard way, but acknowledges these challenges have made her who she is today, including an advocate for vets.

The first and greatest source of healing for Griffith was IAVA because it gave her a unit like the one she had in Iraq, but much better. IAVA is made up of people with different backgrounds and experiences, but with a common purpose: advocating and empowering veterans. Most of the members have open minds about women in combat, and Griffith is able to engage in educated conversations on a wide range of topics affecting post–9/11 veterans. She doesn't feel that sense of hostility that pervaded her unit in Iraq. She described her IAVA team at Storm the Hill as an "all-star team" and is closer to the members of IAVA than most of those with whom she deployed. "IAVA has given me that unit I was looking for in Iraq," she said.

On her first trip to D.C. in 2013, Griffith met another female vet and IAVA member, Rachel McNeill, who is also from Wisconsin and happened to be her roommate all week. McNeill was a student at Harvard. Griffith had dropped out of college and was underemployed. The two instantly clicked. "Shit, if she can do it, so can I," Griffith said. "I've gotta keep up with everyone else." She started college in 2010 but wasn't getting regular VA education payments. This forced her to put her education on hold.

Griffith, an early member of IAVA, was aware of the organization because her dad was a member, and she often referred to IAVA to learn about issues affecting her dad while he was deployed. Then, when she saw *The Real World: Brooklyn* with Ryan Conklin, a soldier who served in Iraq, she thought, "Holy cow. These guys [IAVA] are really different." She's also a member of the Women Marines Association, Team Red, White & Blue, Disabled American Veterans (DAV), and Team Rubicon, an American nongovernmental organization (NGO) founded by U.S. Marines Jacob Wood and William McNulty. Its first mission was in Haiti, a mission the late Clay Hunt had taken part in. "We're so good at what we do in and out of the military so it makes sense to align with each other and do good through organizations that encourage that behavior," Griffith said of her counterparts.

She volunteered with IAVA to get the latest information out to veterans of all generations. She shared what she learned on social media with friends throughout the country and those deployed overseas. She didn't want them to have to take three and a half years to find information like she did. Griffith had had no idea where to begin or whom to contact when she wanted to apply for education benefits; she got into school after finding IAVA's new GI Bill Checklist and Benefits calculator during a Google search.

In 2014, Griffith earned the role of a Leadership Fellow with IAVA. The goal of the fellowship is to have the vets who stormed the Hill take the lessons they learned on Capitol Hill back to their communities.

Griffith likes IAVA because it knows how to cater to the twenty-first-century veteran. She has represented IAVA at Green Bay Packer games, NASCAR races, their Heroes Gala in New York City, and several monthly events in Wisconsin. IAVA says it has her back, and she believes it. They empower veterans to excel— to be students, to work, to do outreach, to find their path in life post-military. After she became a fellow, IAVA rolled out a feature allowing the fellows to peer-verify other veterans who were in Iraq and Afghanistan.

IAVA is a big part of what Griffith has been doing, but it isn't all. She was at Storm the Hill in 2013 when she got a call from a state agency for a job interview. She persuaded the agency to reschedule her interview for the following Monday morning. Though she did not receive that position, she was asked instead to come in and talk to the leadership about Storm the Hill.

The man she talked to took her résumé and business card. She got a job using a noncompetitive hiring authority for qualified veterans rated 30 percent or more disabled, and was appointed to a team lead position in the department's call center for all veterans and family members in Wisconsin. This was her first full-time job since she left the Marine Corps.

Five months later she was promoted to senior outreach specialist. Her job was to take input from nearly 400,000 state veterans on how to better meet their needs. She networked with veterans in rural Wisconsin, where they may not have known they had earned certain benefits. "It makes my day when I help people find what they were looking for and help them improve their quality of life," she said. "Friends say, 'I see you do a lot with the VA. Can you help me get into school?' That's rewarding and it happens quite a bit." In one instance, she helped a veteran she knew from her hometown of Wittenberg, Wisconsin.

She talks of networking, keeping track of other Marines she served with, watching how one another evolves, and going out there and getting it done. "You have something that other people don't have," she said. "You have the veteran card, and you have to go out there and be awesome with it."

Griffith recalled a Marine who went to Iraq and then returned to his rural home in Wisconsin. He has a wife and two children, was working for a waste disposal company, and was unsatisfied with his job. He had been an all-star mechanic in the Marine Corps and now he was crawling under hot garbage trucks, working lots of hours and making a small salary. He liked what he did but he didn't like the conditions. It made her sad to see him unhappy. Griffith found him a heavy equipment mechanic job at the company 3M. It was a union job with good money, so he was better able to support his family.

Another time, parents of a rural Marine came to an outreach event where Griffith was working. The son worked in a restaurant and made very little money. Griffith became Facebook friends with him and connected him with the veteran service officer in his county.

In addition to IAVA helping Griffith out, there is also the network of female veterans in Wisconsin. She had never thought of being separate or different from her male counterparts in the Marine Corps. Male or female, a Marine is a Marine. Still, she was relieved to learn Wisconsin has thousands of female veterans. The women veterans in Wisconsin band together and have a giant unit of their own. When she moved back to Wisconsin, Griffith didn't immediately see herself as a veteran. Her grandfather, her dad, and even her brother—they were vets. It wasn't until she went to the 2010 Wisconsin Women Veterans Conference at Fort McCoy that she realized it: She was a veteran. Her dad, who works at Fort McCoy, had reached out to Gundel Metz, then the women veterans coordinator for Wisconsin. Griffith remembers her dad telling her, "I will pay your way. You're going."

Griffith met Metz first thing on her arrival and then took a seat for the reception. Sitting alone, Griffith was approached by two women, Miranda Cross-Schindler and Bobbie Kolehouse; Miranda is an Army veteran, and Griffith would later take Kolehouse's seat on the Women Veterans Committee. She remembers seeing a small group of loud, boisterous women in the corner of the reception, members of the only chapter of the Women Marines Association in Wisconsin.

"That was a huge turning point for me," she said. Back in 2010, she was on her own, underemployed, and not going to school. She applied for and used FoodShare benefits (food stamps) for the first time in her life. She didn't know how she would make it from one week to the next. Then the female veteran community came to her aid. The female veterans, most of them older than Griffith, took her under their wings and mentored her. Social media helps her stay in contact with the women when they aren't together.

Being a Marine and having good staff NCOs taught Griffith how to have a voice and not be stepped on. Having a voice and giving others the opportunity has helped Griffith heal. "Every time I get to help a vet find a resource, that's very therapeutic," she said. "I love connecting people."

In the summer of 2014, Griffith's journey got a little rocky. A film crew came to her hometown, followed her around for a weekend, and asked a lot of personal questions. It was a great experience, but she was talking about her service in places where she had never talked about it—at a hometown restaurant in Wittenberg with her mother, grandmother, and two great-aunts; at her friend's pool party; at a ball game; at her favorite pub, Limericks Public House. And in her grandma's living room and kitchen, with the clocks taken down and the refrigerator unplugged to limit background noise. It was a great experience, but looking back on it, she realized that answering questions she usually left for the VA became overwhelming. Her two lives collided in front of her family and friends, and it was unsettling. Much of her transition has been in the public eye, and she began to feel like she was doing everything for everyone else and not enough for herself.

Between working for the State of Wisconsin and volunteering for IAVA, Griffith got run-down. She told her leadership at work that she was tired, but they didn't take her seriously. The way they treated her reminded Griffith of her command in Iraq. Her supervisors at her state job were all retired senior leaders with leadership styles very similar to her chain of command in Iraq. One even told her that he knew she had PTSD and had served in Iraq, but that this wasn't Iraq and she needed to get over it. Nobody in that leadership team had ever been to Iraq.

She struggled with the fact she could do so well outside of work in her advocacy efforts, but in her state job as an outreach specialist she was seen as inexperienced, even as a loose cannon. She often questioned herself at work: "How could I go to the White House and make appearances in all sorts of media, and [then] come here and not be trusted to run the registration for an outreach event or talk about what Wisconsin's post–9/11 veterans want to the very people asking how to do a better job for them?"

On her last day at WDVA, they gave her an award in which they spelled her name wrong, and even stated she was in Iraq and Afghanistan (she was only in Iraq). It was a sign of the disconnect between her and the leadership. She smiled and accepted the award, but it will never be placed on her "I love me" wall, where servicemembers hang their honors, awards, pictures, and decorations they receive in the military; instead it will sit in storage. "If this is how agencies responsible for helping Wisconsin veterans operate internally, I don't want anything to do with them," Griffith said. She had seen enough.

When she went for her annual appointment at the VA hospital in Madison, she was there for three hours. When they asked about her mental health, she broke down. She began going to a counselor and enrolled in cognitive processing therapy (CPT). The counselor was someone she had worked with previously when she was on the outreach team, and Griffith had sent vets to her in the past. Now she was the patient in an intense twelve-week CPT course. Griffith has learned that it's okay to be selfish when it means taking care of yourself. It's okay to say, "This isn't what I want or what I was looking for." It's okay to change your mind any time you want. CPT taught her that it's important to be aware of your thoughts, feelings, and emotions.

When she mentioned on Facebook that she was going through CPT, several veterans, male and female, reached out to her. They checked in or encouraged her on a weekly basis. One even had the appointment slot after her. They'd cross paths in the elevator or waiting room and exchange high-fives and hugs. A fellow Wisconsinite and Army veteran, Sara, her roommate at Storm the Hill 2014, became an anchor. The two would chat several times a week. Sara even sent her flowers on her last day of CPT. Griffith believes it was the people who reached out to her and acknowledged her pain that helped her cross the finish line of CPT.

She used to struggle for an answer when people asked her what she did for fun or in her free time. "What free time?" she'd ask jokingly. As if being busy all the time was a sign of importance. She had lost interest in the things she used to enjoy, which is a question she answered on the weekly questionnaire called a PCL-5, a self-report measure that assesses symptoms of PTSD. She became so wrapped up in other people's lives that she didn't leave any time for her own.

After completing CPT, Griffith started to protect her time. She would not get involved in things unless she really wanted to. She took up snowshoeing, started writing her own blog, and pledged to take more time for recess—to find a balance between work and play.

She continued to work in Madison for a few more months. Then, in May 2015, Griffith went to work for the Department of Agriculture as a country of origin labeling reviewer. It required her to travel around northeast Wisconsin and allowed her to move out of the city and back to central Wisconsin, where she felt she belonged. It was a pay cut of nearly ten dollars an hour, but it was a perfect opportunity. It would hold her over until the fall, when she would attend college full-time to study public relations at University of Wisconsin–Stevens Point, using Chapter 31 benefits from the VA.

She was excited about starting school again. When she was fresh out of the Marine Corps, she went to college for a year and a half but didn't graduate. That was what everyone was doing and she had hopped on the bandwagon. Now, at thirty, she was returning as a second-time nontraditional student. Having taken time off from school, worked full-time, and moved several times, she realized it was time to do something truly for herself. She had all the real-world experience but needed the degree to back it up.

Her advice to those returning from service is to move at your own pace. Her dad often tells her, "If you don't take care of Number One, who will?" A lesson well learned.

There's more. "Be aware of what you are feeling," she said. "Realize you are going to have to take care of yourself; there are no corpsmen, no S-1 to do paperwork, and no rent-free living in the barracks. You have got to be your own best advocate in everything you do. Don't be afraid to ask for help, and don't wait to do it. Learn to make time for peace and quiet. Whether it's going to a bookstore, getting out on the water, or blogging, you are feeling a lot and learning a lot. Take care of yourself, because nobody else is going to do it for you."

Soldier Up

Sgt. Viviana Marcotte

SGT. VIVIANA MARCOTTE WAS FLYING HOME ON A COMMERCIAL plane, on leave from the war in Iraq. Dressed in her desert uniform, she found her seat in the back of the plane, tried to get comfortable, and grabbed an in-flight magazine from the seat pocket in front of her. Flipping through it, she found the page containing a map of the world. Marcotte wanted to see where she had been and where she was going.

As she scanned the magazine, she noticed the man sitting next to her was staring at her. He started asking her questions: "What's it like there?" "What did you do?"

If she could have sprinted to the front of the plane, she would have. Instead, Marcotte got up, walked to the front, and, visibly shaking, told a flight attendant, "I need to sit next to those two men in uniform." The airline accommodated her. When she sat down, she grabbed one of the soldier's arms and didn't let go. She didn't know them. All she knew was that they were in uniform and probably also on leave. The soldier gave her a look of understanding.

"I was really anxious," Marcotte recalled. "Everyone was the enemy except for those two in front." She felt on alert, violated. She was having feelings that she couldn't control and didn't understand at the time. "Looking back, I get it," she said.

As Marcotte sank into her seat, maybe she thought about the reasons why she joined the Army and the decisions that led to where she was that day, on her way home from war. Marcotte became a soldier because she wanted to travel and to be part of something bigger than herself. She was also swayed by the GI Joes that she played with as a youngster and by the conversations between her and her stepfather, who had served in the Chilean Army. She also apparently responded to the television commercials that promised "Be all you can be," because one day Marcotte called the number on the ad without telling her parents.

The next thing she knew, she was headed to a recruiting station and enlisting. She was seventeen when she joined the reserves. She went through boot camp her junior year in high school and upon graduation went to advanced individual training (AIT) to become a clinic administrator.

On 9/11, Marcotte had already graduated from high school and was going to drill. Before the plane hit the second tower, Marcotte got a call to report to Fort Devens, a U.S. Army base in Massachusetts. It took a while to hit her, to realize what was happening, but by the end of the day she knew everything was changed.

No one in her unit deployed right away. Marcotte started her bachelor's degree and was halfway through school when she got the call to deploy to Iraq. She started to receive calls from her unit in 2004. They wanted to know if she had everything in order. Then she got "the call" from the commander of her reserve unit. "I don't know how to tell you this, but you've been activated to Iraq, not with us but with another unit that needs your job filled. Oh, and you have four days to report to them. I'm sorry."

Typically you aren't given a short span of four days to pack and get on the plane. It's more like six months' notice. But the military has a policy called "cross-leveling," which means transferring people to a place of immediate greater need. If they need your job and don't have anyone else to fill it, they pull someone from another unit, even if it means short notice. "My life of parties, hanging out with friends, shopping, and other superficialities was now a distant memory," Marcotte said.

Another flight stands out for Marcotte. It's the one she took into Iraq. She heard pinging sounds beneath the plane, like they were being shot at, and the pilot immediately descended. There was a lot of tension, and some on the plane weren't taking it well. An incredible peace came over Marcotte. She knew she had a part to play on this enormous mission. Her goal was to be a light in the darkness.

On paper, Marcotte was a clinic administrator. Her job was to watch over the medical clinic, travel with clinicians, and ensure everything was coordinated with the command. She secured soldiers' medical files, kept statistics and demographics up to date, and published a newsletter. Technically, she wasn't a "counselor," but she was a peer counselor for up to ten Marines and soldiers a day. Peer counseling was an additional duty outside of her clinical administration position. Marcotte said the day she officially fell in love with aiding the mental health of needy soldiers was on her second day with her new unit at Fort Dix. She reported for a brief training at 5:00 A.M. Marcotte walked in and saw everyone lying on the ground. The lights were dim, and an "Affirmations and Stress" CD was playing in the background. She was confused and asked the person next to her what was going on. "We're a combat stress-control unit. We're learning different techniques that we can pass down to soldiers and Marines on the front lines to help them cope with their PTSD." That day, Marcotte learned she was part of a mental health unit, and it changed her then and forever.

Throughout the next fifteen months, Marcotte worked closely with the social workers and psychologists who were counseling the troops coming into the clinics. She absorbed everything she could about the importance of listening to their needs, making sure she was looking for signs of suicidal thoughts, and teaching them coping skills to help them make it through their deployment. Marcotte also taught communication, time management, and anger management classes.

Most of Marcotte's peer counseling dealt with relationship issues back home or how to cope with a difficult leader within a unit. Often the soldiers who came to see her would tell her more than they told the psychologists because what they said to Marcotte didn't go in their record. They didn't have to fear that the conversation would hurt their career.

When a soldier came to see Marcotte, she worked on breaking the ice by offering candy or a magazine. Then she established a rapport by just chatting, peer to peer. She heard from another counselor that she had a relaxing effect on the soldiers and that once they had talked to her, they felt more comfortable in their counseling sessions with the clinicians and with approaching others for help.

The conversations weren't easy. Marcotte carries a lot of them in her heart and doesn't talk about them. It was hard sometimes because she would see soldiers who were suicidal and had tried to hang themselves with their bootlaces. There was one nineteen-year-old who stayed in the clinic for three weeks. "I always made sure I had his favorite candy and put it under his pillow," she said. The candy was Twizzlers. She'd secretly watch him find the candy. It cheered him up, even if just for a short amount of time. He had issues back home, and other soldiers didn't respect him because he was small and quiet. He'd seek out Marcotte and vent about his day, about the bullshit he had to go through. When he left Iraq, he hugged her, cried, and said thank you. He told her she was like an "angel in hell." She let the soldier know that his experience in Iraq didn't have to define him. That this too shall pass. Marcotte has since had angel wings tattooed on her back.

Women soldiers were hesitant to go to the clinic because they were trying to uphold an image that they were strong and resilient, that they could function in a war zone without problems. They didn't want to talk to anyone. They were the toughest to get through to.

The toughest of all were the female gunners and the women attached to the infantry. They were the toughest in good and bad ways. They were on full alert and resilient, which is good. But they wouldn't accept help. Marcotte was thrilled on the rare occasion that a woman did seek her out. "It was beautiful to see them let their guard down," Marcotte said, "when they showed their feminine side. Like a girlfriend in a coffee shop, we're still women."

Marcotte recalls one female gunner who had been sexually assaulted and felt she couldn't go to her command because she believed they would have told her she was weak and transferred her. She loved her job. To make matters worse, back home her husband bailed on their three-year-old son. So she had a lot of emotional and financial stress. And she lost a battle buddy a week prior when a garbage truck blew up in her sleeping compound. The truck hadn't been checked thoroughly at the checkpoint for explosive material.

Marcotte knows she can't "fix people." But she can help. The gunner still had eight months left in Iraq. She wasn't going anywhere soon. Marcotte arranged for more frequent conversations between the gunner and her three-year-old son. She encouraged the gunner to engage in arts and crafts, such as rock painting, and sports like dodgeball. She'd have other soldiers paint on a slab of wood or on a cement wall. One Marine painted a midnight sky with a full moon over the water. He painted his wife, dressed in red and looking out onto the harbor.

Marcotte occasionally held a girls' night where she and the women would use facial cream, clear nail polish, and a paraffin machine to dip their hands in hot wax. They'd even put on makeup for an hour or two. It was Marcotte's way of connecting with the women and letting them know that it was safe to talk to her. After one facial night, a staff sergeant said, "OK, ladies, time to put our masks back on." It's so true, Marcotte said. Being in a male-dominant environment, you have to leave your femininity at the door. Men can show emotion, but if women do it's because they're weak or they're on their period. Women have the heavy burden of proving their worth. The girls' nights she organized were an antidote to that burden.

One of the really special moments was when the female gunner realized that just talking to another woman can be helpful. She didn't have to be the tough gunner all the time. When she returned home, the mother and the boy were reunited. Eventually, the gunner got custody of her son, and Marcotte's command talked to the gunner's command. The perpetrator who sexually assaulted her was moved to another unit.

The tour was emotionally challenging not only for the patients but also for Marcotte, who donated time to the combat support hospitals. She saw a lot of fallen soldiers and Marines. Some died while she was getting their information. She'd walk back to the barracks, numb and with blood on her hands and clothes. Being numb protected her from losing it. It helped her sometimes to not talk about the pain of others that she took on. But she knew holding in the pain could lead to isolation. She needed to be careful. She also felt the impacts of nearby mortar blasts and IEDs.

One time Marcotte recognized a soldier who was medevaced by a Blackhawk to the hospital. He had been in the mental health clinic three weeks earlier. This time she was in the hospital when he was brought in, unconscious and bleeding, on a stretcher. His battle buddy, who had fought alongside him in the firefight, was determined to stay next to him as triage rushed him inside. He was running on adrenaline from the fight and didn't seem to care that he had also been shot and was bleeding. He was determined to stay by his friend's side. His eyes were full of despair and hollow. One of Marcotte's assignments in triage was to take down basic information, including demographics and religion. When she asked him his religion, he laughed at her. "Don't ask me about religion," he said. "No God would ever allow this bullshit to happen." She knew the soldier had also been badly wounded, physically and emotionally, and would never be the same. He would have a long healing journey ahead. "Witnessing the desensitization of your generation is heartbreaking," Marcotte said. "It's heartbreaking to see men and women become so jaded and desensitized from war, death, and anger . . . young men and women that are forever changed. Forced to witness death on a daily basis and carry the wounds of war for years after . . . it will affect them and their families for generations."

The soldier on the stretcher had to have his chest split open and his heart manually pumped. The soldier died. Now Marcotte was picking up his uniform, which was covered with blood. After that, she locked herself in the bathroom, cried, and prayed. She talked to an Air Force psychiatrist, who listened to her and prescribed medication for anxiety.

While in Iraq, Marcotte befriended a soldier named Sean Marcotte, who is now her husband. Sean was a counselor and combat medic. They were in the same unit, but as noted earlier she didn't deploy with her original unit, so she didn't get to know him until they reached Iraq. As the days wore on, Sean became more and more protective of Marcotte. When there were mortar attacks, he would make sure she was OK. "At different moments, when we were under attack or in danger, he would run over to my area," Marcotte said. "No matter what issue we were facing, there was always a silent understanding. 'You cover me. I'll cover you.' I think that still exists."

During the deployment, and at about the same time, Sean's grandfather died and Marcotte's father had a heart attack. Neither was allowed to go on leave back to the United States to be with their families. They grieved together. "Emotionally, we got to the point where we relied on each other," she said.

Marcotte spent the first six months in Baghdad and then did community outreach at Camp Liberty, forty-five minutes south of the city. She helped distribute toys and clothes to local orphanages. Being among Iraqi women and children was fulfilling, but it was a bit awkward. She, along with the other females, was observed and watched closely, more so than the men. Marcotte wore pants and weapons and had a confident air about her when she addressed the male soldiers. The Iraqi women were amazed at this attitude of equality.

When she left for Iraq, Marcotte had been working on a bachelor's degree in communications with a minor in psychology. She had been writing for a leisure magazine in Orlando, Florida, interviewing celebrities. Her goal was to be a journalist of some sort. When she came home, she thought that was the most self-centered degree imaginable. She was totally disgusted by the choices she had made before deploying. When she thought of her old self, she felt like she was walking into someone else's life. "That wasn't who I was anymore," she said.

She knew people from memory, but they were all different. All her relationships had changed because she had changed. She was an only child. Sure, her parents got their child back, but it wasn't the same child—she wasn't the same person. Physically she was the same, but emotionally and mentally she was someone else.

It even took Sean a while to penetrate the wall Marcotte had built between herself and others. "I wasn't in a good place," she said. "I needed to be alone for a while, but Sean didn't listen. He helped me realize I was dealing with more than just some minor isolation. I was struggling with substance abuse and depression, and he insisted I go to counseling."

It took a while after they returned home for Marcotte and Sean to realize they belonged in a relationship and not just a friendship. Even now, if one of them is in a space where they are overly anxious, the other one will help him or her out. "We have a quiet understanding of each other's trauma," Marcotte said, adding that to this day they look out for each other. Sean also faced issues transitioning back, but soon found his place and became a paramedic and a firefighter in Needham, Massachusetts.

Aside from Sean, it would take about three and a half years for Marcotte to start healing and to have a healthy relationship with her family and friends. She lost a lot of friends during that time. What really helped was talking to a veteran officer who had served in Vietnam. He basically told her that if she didn't take care of herself, it was just going to get worse. "Soldier up," he told her. "Help other vets like you were doing in Iraq."

Marcotte has found healing through volunteering and through work. The first year back home is a blur; she calls it "the dark ages." She finished her bachelor's degree, became isolated, started abusing drugs. She was living in a shadow of paranoia.

It was different being in Baghdad, she explained. They had let a lot of Iraqi civilians into the military compound to find employment. She'd see them standing on the roof of a building and staring down at her. She wondered why they had such access. One day, as she was walking through the streets with her team, a group of men began yelling at her and her battle buddy, and moved toward her. "Being a woman in Iraq is tough, especially as a soldier," she said. "They don't feel women have the right to speak or look at men straight in the eye. So you can imagine the power struggle there. Also, being stared at from all angles and wondering what they're scheming all the time makes you constantly vigilant and paranoid." The year 2005 was a difficult one in Iraq. There were a lot of mortar attacks. When she arrived home, Marcotte was scared to be around vehicles for a long time, lest they be rigged with an IED. And she avoided people with coats, who could be packing explosives. She knew it was irrational, but the fear she felt was certainly real.

But then she began volunteering at a veterans shelter and working part-time. The shelter offered her a case management position for Vietnam vets. Marcotte held that job until the grant ran out. Then she got a job in employment training with the Department of Workforce Development as the veteran employment representative. But that wasn't what she wanted to do. She really wanted to work with female veterans.

Speaking from personal experience, Marcotte knows women veterans are a population that rarely receives recognition. She slowly but surely began realizing where the holes were for women in the system. And those holes are what she wanted to focus on.

A coworker recommended her for the position of director for a women veterans network, a program in Massachusetts that Marcotte has been doing since 2010. In this position, Marcotte coordinates events throughout the state specifically for women veterans and travels the state educating the civilian population about women in the military. She reminds the public that every twenty-two minutes a soldier commits suicide. And she personally understands these issues because it took her a long time to find her place in the world when she returned from Iraq.

She also lets the public know about the unique needs and transitional issues women veterans face. Women veterans are four times more likely to be homeless than their male counterparts. Their divorce rate and suicide rate are higher. Their need for child care is great.

"Being around vets eased my anxiety," she said. Marcotte was back in the same capacity as she was overseas. She was actually working with vets who were dealing with the same stuff she was dealing with, only they had been dealing with it for much longer. She even had the honor of helping women veterans of other wars—World War II, Desert Storm, and Vietnam—who are still struggling with PTSD and other traumas. It is her hope that by helping the vets now, they won't become the new Vietnam–era veterans, those who were simply cut loose when their time was up. But they have to push through together.

Being a veteran peer has been tremendously healing for Marcotte. She provides direct assistance, which means she will meet a woman veteran at a coffee shop or go to the home of a military family that isn't aware of what's happening emotionally with their wife or daughter. Some families aren't aware of their benefits simply because they don't know the language. Marcotte, a first-generation born in the United States from Colombian parents, also visits Hispanic military families who need benefits information translated from the English flyers and brochures, as well as cultural empathy. It's rewarding to Marcotte to explain to the family that she was there, in Iraq. She is proof that there is a light at the end of the tunnel. And she directs them to the multi-tude of resources available in Massachusetts.

"I love helping my sister veterans," Marcotte said. "The truth is, women have been sacrificing life and limb for centuries. In the end, the stats and opinions don't matter. What matters is our own individual stories of how women have overcome trauma and continued to heal."

"I can honestly say that our time in the military had its ups and downs, but I wouldn't trade it for anything," she said. "It was the best and sometimes the worst of times for me, but I carry with me the men and women I met, helped heal, made smile, and even a best friend who I made and now call my husband and my biggest supporter in life. Out of the ashes always comes beauty, and that's the message I always hope to pass along to the sisterhood."

Titanium Spirit

Cpl. Amber Lynn Fifer

Date: May 10, 2012
Time of day: Afternoon
Location: Helmand Province, Afghanistan

MARINE CPL. AMBER FIFER WAS PART OF A FEMALE ENGAGEMENT team (FET) that attached to 2nd Battalion, 5th Marines, in Helmand Province. The twenty-year-old from Parker, Colorado, and other Marines set up a vehicle checkpoint in a dried-up river, better known as a wadi, to inspect cars, trucks, and motorcycles coming through the area. Fifer stood post once the night of May 10 and didn't get much sleep.

The next morning, May 11, Fifer was up by 6:00. She got dressed, ate her MRE, brushed her teeth, put on her gear, and checked vehicles for a few more hours. Then it was time to return to the forward operating base (FOB) in the Musa Qal'ah district center.

Around noon, the Marines headed out. They got to a village at the top of a hill when Fifer's truck hit a 70-pound IED. The blast blew the right front tire into a poppy field 30–40 meters away. The explosion demolished the truck's engine. Vehicle parts were strewn all over. While some Marines searched the area for other IEDs, a corpsman performed a post-IED check on Fifer and those in her vehicle to make sure they were okay. Everyone passed. But now they would have to wait for the explosive ordnance disposal (EOD) crew to clear the site and for a mounted patrol to pick up the Marines so they could be transported back to base in another motor vehicle.

The village where they hit the IED had been evacuated the day before. After the explosion, the Marines, Fifer included, went to a nearby compound to ensure there weren't any stragglers still in the village. If they found people left behind, this would give them a better idea of who had planted the IED. The village was deserted except for one family: a man, his two wives, and ten children. The Marines suspected the family was responsible because they were the only ones left. What other possible good reason could they have had for staying behind? They must have planted the IED, because it hadn't been there the day before when the Marines arrived.

The family shouted, "The Taliban did this! The Taliban did this! We hate the Taliban!" This was awkward, Fifer said. Most don't speak out against the Taliban for fear of reprisal. The children and wives seemed distant, like they were hiding something. Perhaps they feared they were in trouble.

The Marines had searched the poppy field abutting the vehicle and road following the IED explosion and found nothing. After they detained and searched the Afghan man, higher Headquarters told them they didn't have enough evidence to prove he was responsible for planting the IED, so the small team who had been detaining and questioning him released him. "There was a miscommunication over the net, and our truck didn't realize he was now heading back to his compound," Fifer recalled.

When he reached the poppy field, he squatted down as if to sit, unburied an AK-47, and opened fire on the downed vehicle. The Afghan shot and killed a Marine outside the truck. Bullets hit Fifer's right bicep, her right and left wrists, and the back of both of her legs. The Marine in the turret, Lance Cpl. Brock Andrew, was shot in his femur. Marines returned fire and the fight quickly ended.

Fifer was in the backseat. The Marine in the driver seat was a combat veteran. He laid Fifer on the ground to assess her wounds and applied tourniquets wherever necessary. The medevac helicopter arrived within fifteen minutes. Fifer and Andrew were taken to Camp Eddy, where a corpsman on site took care of them before they were flown to Landstuhl Hospital in Germany and then to the States.

At Landstuhl, Fifer was heavily sedated and in a relaxed state. She remembers the care from the nurses being "out of this world. . . . They treated us as if we were angels from heaven," she said. "I wish I could reach out and tell each one of them thank you from the bottom of my heart and show them how much better I am. What they did for us was really incredible."

She stayed at Landstuhl for two to three days. Then she was flown to Texas, and finally to Balboa Hospital in San Diego. She was there for four months. Her first surgery was on May 16, 2012. She was in the operating room for eighteen hours. She has four plates and an unknown number of screws in her body. She had a wire/bracket installed in the knuckles on her left hand. She had laser surgery, plastic surgery, and spent a lot of time with orthopedics.

When she was wounded, the events occurred so fast that Fifer couldn't keep up with what was happening. All she could think was, *What just happened? Was I hit? Is everyone ok?* She felt like she was having a crazy out-of-body experience. It was overwhelming and unreal.

The reality of the firefight didn't hit her until she was lying in her bed at Balboa. The doctor asked her if she could feel them touching her right arm, and she couldn't feel anything. She thought he was playing a joke on her. The reason she couldn't feel anything in her right arm was because her radial nerve went into shock when the round impacted her humerus, a condition called nerve palsy, aka paralysis of the nerve. Luckily, the nerve was not severed, so after about a year and a half—and with an extensive amount of occupational and physical therapy—her nerve regenerated.

At Balboa, when she saw her family, reality set in. "When your families' lives come to a screeching halt and they are immediately by your side, it can quickly put the seriousness of things into perspective," Fifer said.

She felt fortunate that her family and friends came to be with her when she was going through so much. "I am so blessed to have such a wonderful support group. Especially since I realize there are some wounded military members who don't come home to that. I am eternally grateful for their love and support," she said.

She had nerve palsy in her right hand that caused her to lose not only the ability to write, but also the ability to do anything for herself that involved the use of her dominant hand. She would have to learn how to write again. In the meantime, she became quite adept at writing with her left hand.

Her last surgery was in 2013. While Fifer was going through the surgeries and healing, she went into survival mode. She described the experience of being wounded as surreal. She never asked, "Why me?" She didn't mope and she didn't feel sorry for herself. She went through it the best she could. She knew she had to use all the strength in her body and mind to get better.

She was in an extreme amount of pain most of the time. Nerve pain in her bicep hurt the most. Fifer couldn't use her arm for a year and a half until the nerves and muscles began functioning again. She went through a lot of physical therapy and occupational therapy at Balboa and Camp Pendleton. "As long as you do what they say, you're going to recover," Fifer said. Each month she could do a little more. She was in a wheelchair for the first two months of her recovery. For such an active person, that was difficult. She felt stuck. Getting out of the wheelchair was a slow process. In the meantime, she did become good at using the wheelchair and learned to continue on with her life.

One time she went to a baseball game and was in so much pain that she had to leave early. There were other times when the pain was so overwhelming it stopped her in her tracks. The pain ranged from a twinge to an attack. When the pain was at its worst, she couldn't think about or do anything else. And it was sporadic. She never knew when it would happen, but she did have medication if she needed it.

She had plastic surgery on her left leg toward the end of her surgeries. It helped how she looked, and more importantly it helped how she felt about her leg. The wound had left a large depression in her leg, with the hamstring sitting up against the skin. A plastic surgeon put fatty tissue from other parts of her body behind the muscle.

After four months at Balboa, Fifer moved into the wounded warrior barracks at Camp Pendleton. These barracks are a battalion-type structure that houses Marines who must be near the hospital and those who need medical attention or treatment so often that they can't really contribute to a regular unit. Residents include people under constant medical care and those in vehicle accidents, wounded in combat, or fighting cancer.

The barracks housed Fifer in handicap-accessible lodging. She stayed there for nine months while she continued treatment. She was in the wounded warrior program from 2012 to 2014 and, as part of her rehabilitation, she exercised by running on an underwater treadmill at Camp Pendleton.

Fifer never wanted to leave the Marine Corps, so she augmented her rehabilitation with running and swimming. She could have chosen to go on permanent light duty but she wouldn't go that route. Eventually, she wants to become a drill instructor (DI), one of the most challenging positions in the Marine Corps.

"There aren't a whole lot of things Marines who are female can do to be at the top of the pack, but drill instructor is one of them," Fifer said. She believes she can meet the requirements it takes to be a DI. She just has to be more careful now. She prepares for the role daily.

In 2013, Fifer moved to Camp Lejeune in Jacksonville, North Carolina. She ran a half marathon that year. To help her heal, she began using a recumbent bike. Then she began swimming at Camp Lejeune. She had to be careful to not put too much strain on her legs. Upper-body exercises like swimming were hard but didn't hurt her body, which was a relief. Putting a lot of strain on herself caused large amounts of nerve pain.

Fifer has always liked to run, but with the aches and pains it's different now. She can't just stretch after she runs, get a good night's sleep, and expect to wake up and feel fine the next day. It may take a week for the pain from running to subside. She constantly has to figure out the right thing for her body. Give and take, trial and error. Make adjustments. This can be time-consuming and frustrating.

One exciting part of her recovery is her ability and enthusiasm to help others. When she works with junior Marines, she can share her experiences with them—along with the need to exercise certain muscle groups. When Marines are under her care, she loves how her life experiences help her lead. Her injuries have taught her a lot about human anatomy and how to properly exercise without getting hurt. This knowledge is a plus in the Marine Corps because Marines are expected to exercise and stay in shape.

It was hard for Fifer when she couldn't go out and be a Marine. During her two-year recovery, she was still expected to wear her uniform and perform basic Marine tasks, such as completing annual training requirements. Yet she wasn't in charge of anything. She had no responsibility except to go to her hospital appointments and to get better. Although this was essential to her healing, it often left her feeling like she was "missing out" on everything that was happening in the world around her. She was sitting on the sideline—on a very slow healing schedule—as the Marine Corps continued to progress without her. She felt like she was accomplishing none of her Marine Corps goals of personal growth and adventure. One particular challenge during her recovery was watching her friends return from Afghanistan and seeing them receive assignments to new units. Not only was she sad to see them leave, she also felt stuck in the wounded warrior battalion. She knew she still had a long way to go and a lot more progress to make until she could get back to fleet Marine Corps.

Fifer wasn't used to letting other people help her, so another part of her healing was learning to accept the help of others. "It's very humbling," said Fifer, who at first couldn't do anything without help. She couldn't wash herself, wipe herself, comb her hair, or scratch her leg or arm. She couldn't sit up on her own.

She couldn't put on her own ChapStick—and that part drove her especially crazy.

"I had to ask for everything," she said. "Please move my arm a centimeter to the right or left, so I can be more comfortable"; or "Please wipe my nose because I'm feeling congested." The hardest part was having just been so independent and now being in a position where every single thing had to be done for her. "If I was lucky, it would be a family member who I was comfortable with," she said. "But often it was a random nurse who I'd never met. They were given the task to take care of me, and even though they were so gentle and sweet, it didn't make the fact that a random stranger was bathing me or wiping my nose any less embarrassing."

She didn't experience any specific low points or extreme feelings of depression. It was mainly a roller coaster of emotions. Surgeries were spaced about four to five months apart. This meant that around three months, when she was beginning to feel like her old self again and making progress in her running, she would start back at square one. The medications made her feel extremely sick and lethargic; by about the third month post-surgery, she would be taking the least amount required to manage pain, which allowed her to feel more alert and less sick. The medications also drastically changed her body. Some made her sick to her stomach, making it difficult to keep food down, so she lost a lot of weight. She lost 20 pounds just from the transport from Afghanistan to California. Her weight continued to fluctuate, and the medications wreaked havoc on her immune system. While she was undergoing major surgeries, she got sick frequently. A common cold easily turned into the flu, and she would be in and out of the emergency room with a high fever.

All of this was very taxing and caused a lot of stress. She began to experience chest pain and had to be admitted for an ultrasound and heart exam so they could ensure she wasn't reacting poorly to the medication—or worse. Luckily, she was okay, and they found nothing wrong with her heart, but it was a scary reminder of how seriously stress can affect you. From then on, she tried to exercise more and tried yoga to relieve stress.

In January 2014, Fifer was accepted for reenlistment and received a lateral move into the geospatial intelligence field. On January 17, she swore in for the second time and, shortly after, checked into the 2nd Intelligence Battalion on Camp Lejeune. Here, she did on-the-job training with intel analysts until April, when she checked into her new schoolhouse aboard Fort Belvoir in Virginia. She went to school for seven months and graduated on November 7, earning the military occupational specialty (MOS) of 0261, Geospatial Intelligence Analyst. She hopes to deploy again one day, to be a drill instructor, and to finish out a twenty-year career as a geospatial analyst.

Riding to Recovery

Airman 1st Class
Sarah Bonner

AT TWENTY-FOUR, SARAH BONNER WAS ON A NEW BASE, IN A NEW city, in a new country. She transferred to Germany in May 2005 to be a financial apprentice and disbursement chief for 435th Comptroller Squadron. Her home would be Vogelweh Air Base and her workplace Ramstein Air Force Base.

The second week she was there, she got her shipment from the States of personal belongings, including her TV and DVD player. She needed to get everything hooked up. Of course it's different in Germany. She would need an adapter and electrical cord, plus just help in general getting herself adapted. She met an Army MP at the base security gate when she forgot her military ID. The next day, she saw the same soldier in the PX (base store). He offered to help her hook up her appliances. He suggested that afterward they get a drink and go to his place to watch a movie. Bonner was a little homesick and looking for someone to hang out with. She was alone in a dorm room in a new country.

She had things to look forward to, but nothing happening right away. They bought the materials to hook up her appliances the next day and decided to go out for drinks instead of a movie.

She was having fun. Bonner had attended a two-year college and been through basic training and tech school, where she had little to no freedom. She had never drunk much, and she sensed a newfound freedom. Drinking was part of the culture in Germany. Bars run by Americans, Germans, and GIs dotted downtown K-town (Kaiserslautern).

She had ended a relationship before she joined the Air Force. She thought maybe she was ready to start dating again. But the guy she was with wasn't so nice, as it turned out. He wanted to drink—a lot. Bonner likes a drink, but she's not that big of a drinker. That night she had a few, but when she reached a point where she felt nearly out of control, she started drinking water. It was 98 degrees and humid. She needed water to cool off.

Then she went to the bathroom. She thought, *He seems like a nice guy. He's an MP. A cop. He's responsible.* She never anticipated what would happen next. While she was in the bathroom, he put a Rufi (rape drug) and Ketamine (horse tranquilizer) in her water.

Then he was getting too touchy-feely. She'd had enough. She didn't want him to go any further. Enough was enough. "I thought he just had a few too many," she said. As they drove back to his house on base, she remembers recognizing the guard at the gate. She doesn't remember much after that. Things went blank. They went to her date's house on Vogelweh. She fell asleep and woke up the next morning in a daze.

She felt as though she had a bad cold. Her nose was stuffy and hurt when she rubbed it, like she had been hit in the face. *What happened?* she wondered. She felt like she wasn't 100 percent awake. Then she saw the blood on her hands and knew something was wrong.

Now she was wide awake. She got up and looked around. Her clothes and the contents of her purse were strewn about. Her rapist lay naked on the floor on the other side of the room with a sheet wrapped around him.

Am I still on base? Am I still in Germany? How long have I been here? Sarah was disoriented. She saw 110- and 220-volt outlets in the room, so she knew she was on an American base. Bonner got dressed. She could tell someone had torn off her clothes because one of the legs of her jeans was partially inside out. She grabbed her purse and keys and got out fast.

Once outside the house, she remembered where she was. She looked at the house number so she would remember where she had been. She walked—ran—to her dorm, about a half mile away, and when she arrived she locked all the doors. It was six or seven in the morning; many of the soldiers and airmen were just coming home from the bars and were angry that the doors were locked.

Bonner grabbed a phone in the hallway, called the base operator, and asked for the chaplain. She's not sure why she called the chaplain first. She just did. The chaplain was kind and understanding. She explained that she was new on base, had only been there for a few weeks, and had just been raped and she didn't know what to do. Bonner didn't even know where the hospital was.

By now she could barely stand. She leaned against the wall while she talked on the phone. The chaplain sent the police and an ambulance to Bonner's dorm. He stayed on the phone with her until the police arrived. An Army MP had just raped her, and when the Army and Air Force MPs showed up, Bonner freaked out. Then fear turned into strength. She picked up a chair and held it over her head when the police tried to unlock the door. She didn't trust them. "If you come through that door, I'm going to throw this chair at you!" she yelled.

They talked her down. When they reached Bonner, the MPs threw her to the ground to protect themselves and to protect her from herself. A security camera caught the images of Bonner entering the dorm and holding the chair over her head. She had a bloody nose and black eyes.

Bonner began to feel everything that had been done to her— where she had been hit, kicked. She asked to be sedated before she lost control on the stretcher. She hadn't looked in the mirror. She hadn't even gone into her dorm room. A female police officer went into her room and got her clothes and toiletries.

The paramedics were concerned she had a head or spinal cord injury. They strapped Bonner onto a backboard to stabilize her so that she wouldn't be a threat to herself or to anyone else. She'd had a prior back injury and the backboard would help prevent further complications, she told the medics. She didn't know that she had several broken ribs and a broken nose and would need stitches.

At the hospital, she met the chaplain in person. He stayed with her through most of her medical care. She doesn't remember when he left. But while still in the ER, Bonner learned that she was one of several women who had been assaulted that night.

Then she was sedated for the medical procedures, including the rape exam. She had been a virgin when she was assaulted. Late in the evening, when her medical treatment was done, Bonner was sore all over.

She was interviewed by the Air Force Office of Special Investigations (OSI) in the ER and by the Army's Criminal Investigations

Department (CID) at their office. A victim's advocate arrived late
at the hospital and drove her to the CID office, but wasn't allowed
to be present for the meeting. CID asked Bonner if she was sure
she and the MP from the bar hadn't simply been roughhousing.
Without actually asking, they suggested that maybe she had been
desperate to find a guy. She felt they were ganging up on her.
The questioning took hours. No one encouraged Bonner to press
charges. The hospital staff asked her if she was going to press
charges, but CID discouraged her from doing so.

Bonner almost felt guilty, as if she'd been in the wrong. "If I
hadn't gone out for a drink, none of this would have happened,"
she told herself.

She was moved to another dorm on Ramstein, which was
better, but the perpetrator still followed her. She'd find notes
on her door from him, and friends would tell her that he had
been in her dorm. Fortunately, she didn't come face-to-face with
him again.

The most immediate help Bonner would get came from the
chaplain. He asked Bonner what she was doing in her spare time.
She was trying to find a church, she said, which opened the door
for the chaplain to recommend different ministries, including
the single airmen ministry. With a support team from the church,
she could go hiking, swimming, and touring, and feel safe doing
it all. They ate meals together one night a week and traveled to
places like the Black Forest in Germany and Strasbourg, France.
She shared what had happened with a group of Christian women.
She was the only one there who was a survivor. It wasn't until she
started talking about the rape that she realized how significant
and traumatic it was.

She also got involved in Cadence International, a hospitality
ministry. They run the Kaiserslautern Hospitality Haus, located

just off base, where Bonner would go on Friday nights for pot-
luck, Bible study, and games. These activities got her mind off
what had happened, got her out of the dorm and into another
safe environment. The chaplain had urged her to find activities
that didn't involve alcohol. Bonner had already gotten herself
into one mess with alcohol. "I never wanted to be in that situation again," she said. By "that situation," she means having fun
but feeling out of control to the point that someone could take
advantage of her.

She kept reaching out to people, getting accustomed to Germany, and enjoying the fact that life gradually got better. Time
heals all wounds. However, she had a lot of anger and a lot going
on in general with learning her job, taking care of her medical
needs, and making friends. Her new commander realized she was
in a bad spot and came to her. Her first commander, the one in
charge when she was raped, was in the reserves and didn't know
how to deal with military sexual trauma (MST). The new commander told her that whatever she needed with regard to mental
health would be available to her.

PTSD symptoms started to present themselves in the form of
nightmares. Bonner would wake up from a nightmare punching
and grabbing at things that weren't there. She'd scratch the
wall. One morning she woke up and found herself sitting on
the floor next to the bed. She was nervous day and night. She
started going to counseling and taking medications to prevent
AIDS and other diseases. While Bonner was trying to put her
life back together, the perpetrator was prosecuted for battery
and harassment.

Fortunately, Bonner doesn't spend much time looking back
and dwelling on her past. She prefers to look ahead. "I've been
able to move on from this," she said. She is very careful about who

she interacts with within the MST community. Many members are stuck in their past, and she doesn't want to be one of them. She doesn't want to drag herself down.

She found a lot of support from a few survivors who encourage and challenge her. One in particular has helped her a great deal with processing her assault as well as learning the role it has played in her recovery and mental health. Bonner went on to get a degree in social work and is learning how to live with the PTSD without it affecting her life and practice. She wants to continue moving forward. It's a process she will have to start and restart throughout her life.

In 2006 she was medically discharged for injuries related to her military service. She had lymphedema in both legs and injuries to her feet.

A month before she officially separated from the military, she returned to the United States from Germany. It was difficult because she returned to an area far from any military bases, to the small town of Lynchburg, Virginia. It turns out Lynchburg was just a bit too small. She served for a total of twenty-six months, not a full enlistment, so everyone she knew before she had enlisted wondered why she was back so soon. When Bonner got home, people recognized her and asked if she was still in the military; she had to explain that she was medically discharged. Explaining what happened got old quickly, as no one seemed to get it. Some people even said that God was punishing her because the military was meant for men, not women. Others said her medical discharge made her a failure as a soldier.

She went back to school. She already had an associate's degree, but had to start over when she decided to get a bachelor's degree in social work; she wanted to help others who had gone through a similar situation.

Given everything she's been through, all the counseling and support, nothing has been as helpful to her as exercise, specifically cycling. In 2011 she got back into riding through the Wounded Warrior Project Soldier Ride. She started riding a three-wheel recumbent bike because of her back injury. After she was fitted for the bike at Walter Reed National Military Medical Center, they almost had to physically pry her off the bike because she loved it so much. It felt like Christmas morning when she got the bike. She had tears of joy because she could finally ride again, and ride pain free! Nothing hurt, and she was actually doing something physically strenuous. She felt in control again. It was an amazing feeling—one she hadn't had in a long time.

Leading up to the Soldier Ride, she started on a stationary bike and took spin classes to train and build her endurance. That prepared her for three days of riding, which included a 35-mile ride through D.C. and a 45-mile ride through Annapolis. The ride began at the White House with a meeting with President Obama.

After the bike ride, she thought, *If I can do this, what else can I do?* Knowing the bike worked for her was empowering. Being able to ride with others and sharing that time with them was extra special. The bike ride helped Bonner believe that anything is possible and that she just needs to find a way to ride a bike and get fit without reinjuring herself. A few months after the ride she learned about CrossFit, a strength and fitness program performed at high intensity, and its full mobility program. She checked it out, not sure what to expect. She was scared about what she had gotten herself into. It proved to be a great opportunity, and she was instantly hooked. Just being able to do the exercises and to be with other people was fun. And she saw the results.

Since her first bike ride in 2011, Bonner has participated in several more, including a three-day Soldier Ride in June 2012 in Chicago and a two-day ride, Face of America through World T.E.A.M. Sports, in 2013 from Arlington to Gettysburg. She didn't finish that one because her bike almost crashed into a tree, stopping two feet in front of it, but she did complete 50 miles the following day, for a total of 76 of the 110 miles. She also rode the Memorial Challenge in 2013 with Ride 2 Recovery on her recumbent bike from Arlington to Virginia Beach.

Cycling continues to be Bonner's primary choice for healing. It's a way to experience freedom and soar to new heights. For a long time, riding an upright bike was not possible because leaning forward caused back pain. But she wanted to challenge herself, and in October 2013 she got back on an upright bike and was successful! She again shed tears of joy. Riding an upright has opened more doors for Bonner, as it is easier to transport and can go just about anywhere.

On the Face of America ride in 2014, the same ride as the previous year, Bonner rode an upright bike and was nervous she would crash again. She used the brakes "like there was no tomorrow," she said. Bonner has learned to trust herself, her bike, and the people around her, to be mindful, and to enjoy the fun of going downhill.

On that same race, she met three other survivors of MST, as well as vets with PTSD and traumatic brain injury (TBI). She also met a social worker who rides with her clients. People talk about things differently when they're on a bike than when they're in the office. This is the kind of social work Bonner would like to do someday—bicycle therapy.

"The bike takes my mind off the PTSD," Bonner said. "Even though I'm disabled, I'm still very able."

In 2014, Bonner was fortunate to receive a new bike through a grant from The Independence Fund, a group that helps wounded veterans and first responders, just in time to ride in the Memorial Challenge. She hopes to do more challenges with Ride 2 Recovery and the Wounded Warrior Project.

"I know the power of bike riding and what it has done for me and for so many other veterans," Bonner said. "I hope to share that with veterans in my area, in the hopes of empowering them and allowing them to experience the freedom I've experienced."

Bonner relates cycling to life. "Bike riding is very much like life, as you must keep looking forward, otherwise you put yourself in danger," she said. "Just as looking back and dwelling on our past often causes us to get caught up in the past, looking behind on a bike puts the rider at risk of falling off the bike or running into other riders. Also, when riding a bike roads and trails change a lot. They can be flat, rough, uphill, downhill, twist, and turn just like life. Life has many twists and turns and ups and downs that we must all navigate and cannot avoid. Such as with riding a bike, you cannot ignore or avoid the hills and difficult paths. It's important that you embrace going downhill and uphill."

Another outlet that has been transformative for Bonner is The Telling Project, which offers veterans the opportunity to tell their stories on stage. Veterans are partnered with actors to perform their stories. Bonner was one of six veterans (the only woman) asked to prepare and rehearse their stories in a week's time in D.C. She performed her story just before the six-year anniversary of the rape. The day before the show, she threatened to leave and not do it. She started second-guessing herself and got nervous and overwhelmed. However, the directors and her fellow castmates refused to let her give up. They knew she needed to share her story, so they worked with her to overcome her fears and find the strength to tell her story. "We're not letting you run," she was told.

"It was terrifying but gave me closure," she said. "It allowed me to share what happened, to take ownership of it, and end it the way I wanted to end it. It felt like I had taken a weight off my shoulders."

After telling her story and sitting down, she remembered to breathe. She looked back at the audience and could see her story had hit them hard. She got emotional at the end, when the cast received a standing ovation. All the cast was there for her and they hugged. She cried. "I shared it and I'm OK," she said. "I survived it." She did the work to get herself through this process. Watching a video of her acting has been therapeutic as well.

"This is my story," Bonner said. "What happened to me sucks." But through it all she found her true calling: She wants to help others who have been silenced by sexual trauma. "What happened to me was wrong, but it doesn't have to define who I am," she said.

In 2013, Bonner worked with Jonathan Wei, founder of The Telling Project, and Michele Hilts, a veteran certifying official and veterans advocate at the Virginia Western Community College, to bring a production to her hometown of Roanoke, Virginia. "The experience of performing my story in D.C. was so powerful that I knew I needed to work to bring this to my hometown. It's often hard for veterans to talk about their experiences, but it's very important to do that. I wanted to help other veterans I know and those that live in my hometown to have the same opportunity I had," Bonner said.

In November 2013, Bonner and two other veterans—one who also experienced MST and the other the spouse/caregiver of a veteran—shared their stories in three performances at Virginia Western Community College. "It was harder than I expected it to be now that I was doing it in front of my hometown," she said. "I went to school there for two years and was very involved in the Roanoke community. The audience knew me."

While it was hard, it was also very powerful and healing. Former and current professors and fellow classmates from Radford University were there and all commended her for bringing The Telling Project to Roanoke and for sharing her story. Only a few of them knew her story in advance, so for many it was the first time they heard what had happened to her. They were impressed with how far she'd come and with how she used her experience to work for change and to help others. After the final performance, she let herself breathe again.

Four weeks after the Roanoke performance was the seventh anniversary of Bonner's separation from the military. Often the anniversary is a bittersweet day for Bonner. She struggled with feelings of anger and frustration and failure. But 2013 was different. "I had finally come full circle and had closure," she said. With the passage of time, years of counseling and therapy, personal growth that allowed her to forgive her assailant, classes on mental health skills, social work classes, and performing her story in her hometown, she found closure. For the first time since she left the Air Force in 2006, she did not regret November 27, the day she got out of the military. Instead, she embraced it and was able to truly enjoy it, which allowed her to appreciate Thanksgiving with her entire family.

Bonner graduated from Radford University in May 2014 and plans to pursue a master's degree in social work. She hopes to start a program to assist veterans making the transition from military life to civilian life and bring it to the VA. She has

interned with Total Action for Progress in Roanoke to help veterans who are homeless get into housing. She also focuses her
attention on working to change the current policies in place for
survivors. She continues to tell her story more as opportunities
present themselves.

Advocate for First Responders

Staff Sgt.
Katherine Ragazzino

IN 2003, MARINE STAFF SGT. KATHERINE RAGAZZINO (RIZZO) went on a convoy transporting Intel from Basra to Al Faw, Iraq. She was providing rear security for a three-truck convoy. When they reached Al Faw, Intel would meet up with recon.

They got to the base in Al Faw and proceeded to take Intel and recon to their outposts at a higher level so the Marines could assess the enemy's activity in a particular area. Once they reached their destination, the convoy took a break. Toward the end of the twenty-minute break, Ragazzino went to the bathroom behind a rock. While she was relieving herself, she heard shots.

Pop! Pop! Pop!

Ambush! They were taking fire.

The transporters, including Ragazzino, quickly got back in their trucks and drove through the firefight, heading back to Basra. Ragazzino, with her M4 rifle in hand, again provided rear security. As the Marines were leaving, Ragazzino was on high alert. She had to be. Iraqis were driving by in vans; they, too, could be armed. She had to be vigilant. During the firefight, Ragazzino wore dark glasses that she hoped prevented the enemy from seeing her—seeing into her soul, that is. "Thank God they couldn't see me," she said. "It was like you were staring into each other's souls. We were in such close proximity [in our vehicles] that we could literally see into each other's eyes."

She was in shock. No one talked about the near-death experience. How do you put it into words? Why bother? Weren't they just doing what they were trained to do?

Originally from Philadelphia, Ragazzino joined the Marines eighteen months after graduating high school. Ragazzino initially worked with administration, but she also became a Marine Corps martial arts instructor—proficient in both lethal and nonlethal tactics—who trained and deployed with special operations–capable units.

She first deployed in 2001 for offshore operations in the Middle East. She returned home and then redeployed as part of a peacekeeping force in 2003–4 to Basra and Al Faw. She participated in offshore operations in the Middle East and off the coast of Afghanistan before going into Iraq, where she was with the 13th Marine Expeditionary Unit Command Element Special Operations Capable (MEUSOC) out of Camp Pendleton, California.

Ragazzino went into Iraq as an administrator but wasn't limited to that role. She volunteered for foot patrols with the male Marines and interpreters, which led to meeting with the local people to inform them that the Marines were there for peacekeeping efforts and humanitarian assistance. This was before there were female engagement teams and the Lioness Program, which attached female Marines to combat units to search Iraqi women and children who might try to smuggle money or weapons through security checkpoints. Women on patrol were extremely rare. Ragazzino's hair was short, hidden by a helmet. She wore glasses that hid her face, as well as a neck gaiter that she used to cover and protect her face from sandstorms. With all that gear, she was hardly distinguishable from the male Marines. Ragazzino chose to go on the foot patrols because she knew she was strong enough to handle that environment, and she was confident in her fellow Marines. They would take care of one another.

That same year, during her 2003–4 deployment, Ragazzino was on her way back to camp in a 5-ton truck when one of the front wheels drove into an eroded fighting hole. Before the truck hit the hole, she noticed a boy flying a kite in a field and other kids playing in the sand. The last thing she remembers was talking to a sergeant. Then she was thrown from the right to the left side of the truck. Her head struck the truck and knocked her unconscious. The accident cracked her skull and caused internal injury. She went to medical later that evening after having dizzy spells and vomiting and learned she had a concussion.

When she returned to Camp Del Mar in California in 2004, Ragazzino entered a very dark period of her life. She hadn't processed the ambush or the truck rolling into a ditch. She hadn't dealt with the physical or emotional impact, including the hatred she felt toward herself. Ragazzino hated her life and every other living thing. "I became someone I wasn't" while in Iraq, she said. "The experience, when you're put in the real shit, is spiritually challenging. This is no game. Every day was so aggressive. I was hypervigilant and impatient. I was all those things."

Friends died in combat, yet she made it home alive. She didn't feel providing rear security in Iraq was significant, that it mattered. She didn't know she had a brain injury. Ragazzino hated what was "boiling inside" her and not being able to assess the situation, assess herself.

Alone in her home in Carlsbad, California, Ragazzino kicked and screamed. Anything in her path was fair game. In fits of anger, she destroyed objects from her childhood, such as drawings and decorations. Where had her innocence gone? Ragazzino had a traumatic brain injury (TBI) but didn't know it. She wouldn't find out about the injury until 2008, after she was hospitalized for physical impairments and PTSD. She was having all sorts of mood swings and physically didn't feel normal either, but she had no idea what was going on.

Ragazzino could no longer handle simple administrative skills, nor could she concentrate or focus. She couldn't put quotation marks around quotes. She lost feeling on the left side of her face and her fingers became numb. And Ragazzino grew distant from everyone. Her impaired vision, lack of concentration, and numbness became so severe that she had to transfer to a non-deployable unit, which only increased her anger.

Just five months after she returned from Iraq, Ragazzino's mother died. That same year her aging and ailing father came to live with her. He was a World War II Marine and Iwo Jima veteran. He was her hero, her reason for joining the Marines. Ragazzino went to every Marine Corps ball with him except when she was deployed.

She had been approved by Headquarters Marine Corps to be put on humanitarian assistance—this overrides a Marine's ability to do most daily Marine Corps duties. This was a difficult time for Ragazzino. She had gone from a special ops unit in Iraq to a non-deployable unit at Marine Corps Base Camp Pendleton. "I had left and come back," she said. "My life had changed so much. We had nothing in common."

While on humanitarian assistance, Ragazzino's unit made it extremely difficult for her to help her dad, and she doesn't understand why. She'd rather not say what they did because she doesn't want to talk negatively about this unit. Ragazzino said there was a lack of senior leadership within her chain of command, but not within the unit as a whole. The Marine Corps wasn't the problem; it was individuals. Ragazzino had always been a model Marine and was one to set the example. She put the Marine Corps first. On her deployments she had excellent senior leadership, which she wanted to emulate. Now, after enduring multiple unforeseen life-changing injuries, Ragazzino felt her new leadership didn't understand her or her PTSD. (She still didn't know about her traumatic brain injury, but she knew she had PTSD.) They had no idea what she was going through.

She couldn't take it anymore. She was prescribed Valium for anxiety and Prozac for PTSD by a doctor at the Camp Pendleton hospital. While she was avoiding opportunities to hurt herself, her company gunnery sergeant asked her to do a weapons count in their armory. She refused to do it and could not understand why they would ask her to do the count when they knew she was on heavy-duty medication.

To her dismay, she overheard those same senior Marines referring to her as a "broken-down car." They didn't get to know her, nor did they ever make an honest effort to address the challenges she faced. They put her in situations that would make any young Marine screw up. They wanted to transfer her from California to a base in North Carolina in the middle of her medical treatment.

A year later, in late 2005, leadership within Camp Pendleton Range Operations stepped in after Ragazzino shared the health problems she was having. They were very helpful and allowed her to go to therapy. They also honored her humanitarian assistance, allowing her to take care of her father at home. During this period, Ragazzino became the first active-duty woman Marine range inspector at Camp Pendleton. She was going to therapy, firing weapons on the range, and happy again.

She continued her therapy, maintained her career, and took care of her father full-time until he died in November 2006. She gave it her all, grateful for the assistance she received from the Marine Corps and compassionate civilians when caring for her father.

Ragazzino was promoted to staff sergeant and transferred to Camp Talega, on the outskirts of Camp Pendleton, where she helped make military IDs for reservists and active-duty service-members. She felt comfortable with the slower pace, like she was back on track again. But after the death of her mother as well as her father, and still not fully understanding the physical and mental changes that had been affecting her since returning home from deployment, Ragazzino started drinking. She was underweight and, it turns out, unstable. She had never abused alcohol before, but now she saw its benefits. It helped her forget about her injuries, numbed her emotionally and physically, and helped her forget about her parents' deaths and her trauma.

Ragazzino continued as a martial arts instructor (her brain injury was still undiagnosed), teaching male and female Marines. She loved the Marine Corps and hoped to stay in as long as she could.

In December 2007, Ragazzino's condition had deteriorated so much that she was transferred to the Naval Medical Center in San Diego. At Balboa Hospital, she was placed in the Comprehensive Combat and Complex Casualty Care (C5) center to help her with the brain injury and post-traumatic stress.

For a year and a half, Ragazzino lived in hospital grounds building #26 with wounded Marines and other servicemembers, receiving daily treatments such as vestibular therapy, cognitive behavioral therapy, physical therapy, and group therapy. She found everything challenging. She was sick and in a dark place.

"I just wanted to be a Marine again but I didn't know how," she said. She loved her career and would do it over again. Ragazzino is proud of her accomplishments. Though she did her best to overcome both cognitive and physical impairments, they eventually proved to be serious and long-lasting.

She was honorably discharged from the Marine Corps and medically retired in June 2009 from Wounded Warrior Battalion West after twelve and a half years of service. Once released from active-duty service, Ragazzino enrolled in the VA and continued her treatment at the VA Polytrauma Center in Palo Alto, California. In mid-2010 she was discharged and returned to the San Diego area.

The year 2010 marked a turning point for Ragazzino. When she was receiving treatment at the Naval Medical Center (from December 2007 to June 2009), the Injured Marine Semper Fi Fund Organization had reached out to her, and she became a core member on Team Semper Fi. She was given a huge opportunity to go on an expedition to Nepal in 2010 with Soldiers to Summits. This opportunity "planted the seed" toward change in her life in a spiritual way that she had never felt before. This journey of healing was filmed in the documentary *Higher Ground,* which was released in 2012.

Unfortunately, the healing got a bit lost in her struggle to get her VA benefits straight. Since her medical discharge from the Marine Corps, Ragazzino had been fighting with the VA for her benefits/finances, which were administratively incorrect after being transferred from the Department of Defense (DoD) to the VA. When she left the care of the DoD (active duty) and transferred to the VA (veteran status), she had hoped the change would be flawless, yet her worst fears came true. She became a victim of the system, a veteran left behind, when her rating was misclassified.

This issue was still ongoing when Ragazzino returned from Nepal. She said she felt like a piece of chewed gum on the pavement: just tossed away, and her taste for life gone. She felt dead inside. Ragazzino didn't feel as though she had anything to come home to, except thoughts of killing herself.

The day she left her hotel to return to San Diego after the expedition to Nepal, Ragazzino had to walk through the hotel's two sets of automatic doors. The first set of doors opened, and she stood in the middle with the doors closing behind her. Someone on the trip had been encouraging to Ragazzino. "Don't ever lose what you have," she was told. "You can change the world." *What do they see in me that I don't see?* she wondered. She paused in this neither-inside-nor-outside world and, as she went through the second door, it was as if she'd left her old life behind. In that moment she didn't quite understand what she was feeling, but she took a deep breath, briefly closed her eyes, and said, "It's going to be a rough road, but you've got this, girl."

"The hardest part of going from victim to being in control of your life is making a commitment to yourself," Ragazzino said. "Looking at yourself honestly." She began to believe in herself again, thanks to people empowering her and having faith in her. "Everyone has the ability to take control of their life," she said. "We can lose this along the way because of what life throws at us, but we can also get it back. Looking within and being able to accept is the hardest part."

With a little money from Social Security disability and the VA, she put her belongings in storage and became homeless for close to a year. She lived out of her vehicle in Point Loma, San Diego. She felt safe there and sought refuge by attending the Rock Church on Sundays.

It was the lowest point of her life, the rock bottom. "I was lost and living in shambles," she said. She had to make a decision at that point that no matter what, she was going to make it. Instead of blaming the trauma on someone else, she made a conscious decision to not let her trauma control her. "You have to allow yourself to go through the process and fall apart," she said.

While she had been hospitalized at Wounded Warrior Battalion West, Ragazzino's case manager and doctors felt a service dog would be helpful for her TBI and PTSD. Six months before she was discharged, Ragazzino got a golden-greyhound service dog named Daisy. Daisy has been there for Ragazzino through her darkest hours, including when she was homeless. She knew they would be okay because they shared a bond. Together they hung out in the park.

During Ragazzino's homelessness, Daisy came first. She was family. The dog ate better than her owner. Daisy was on a vet-prescribed diet and properly cared for. Ragazzino ate mostly pizza and items from fast-food dollar menus. She'd buy canned foods and items at the Dollar Store as well. She slept a lot so she wouldn't have to think about being hungry.

Daisy is a certified service dog in the United States and has been with Ragazzino since her discharge and transfer to the VA, which has its own policies on service dogs. Ragazzino filed two claims but has been denied approval due to the VA's regulations on certification. As of late 2015, Ragazzino was still trying to get Daisy grandfathered by the VA so that the dog's special care will be covered and so that she receives the quality of life she deserves. "She's my lifeline," Ragazzino said.

Daisy alerts Ragazzino when it's time for her to take her medication and when she is having an onset of Bell's palsy. Daisy helps Ragazzino control herself during stressful situations and wakes her from nightmares. She also nudges her owner when there are changes in Ragazzino's body. For instance, if Ragazzino has a migraine coming on, Daisy will sense it before her owner does. "Daisy comforts me and gives me something to be responsible for," Ragazzino said. "She gave me something to live for."

While she was homeless, Ragazzino began to realize what she wanted but didn't know how to get it. She knew her life had value, but she didn't know what that value was. She cried often. She had a DVD player, so she watched movies in her car or watched planes take off and land at San Diego International Airport. And she daydreamed about another life—with a home and a family.

About seven years earlier, in 2004, Ragazzino had met Michelle Tyler, a licensed vocational nurse and the wife of Ragazzino's former staff noncommissioned officer. Tyler assisted Ragazzino with caring for her father until his passing. She was also concerned with Ragazzino's health and well-being. Tyler's advocacy for Ragazzino started while she was in Balboa Hospital; Tyler visited her often. Upon her discharge, however, Ragazzino distanced herself from everyone, including Tyler. She continued to struggle with the VA for full benefits and with the loss of her career. Sometime later, Ragazzino was in a YouTube clip for the *Higher Ground* documentary. Tyler saw the clip and tracked down her friend to the parking lot where Ragazzino was living out of her vehicle. Tyler told her that she wasn't going to be homeless on her watch. "You're coming home with me," she said. It was now August 2011.

Ragazzino moved in with Tyler. Over the next year, they worked on her physical and emotional health as well as her overall quality of life. Tyler became Ragazzino's VA caregiver and helped her get off some medications and manage the ones she still needed.

Within two weeks of moving in with Tyler, Ragazzino and Tyler went to see their congressman, Bob Filner, to find out if he could help Ragazzino with her disability rating and general services. Ragazzino requested a review of all her service-connected conditions from her time of discharge. The VA personnel present at the meeting acknowledged that Ragazzino's claim had clearly fallen through the cracks in the system. That day the VA put a Band-Aid on the wound, which was helpful but didn't address the underlying issue. At the end of the meeting, a VA representative from the San Diego regional office said to give the VA six to nine months to get Ragazzino's rating claim with outstanding issues resolved. Filner said to contact him if they needed anything else.

In October 2012, Tyler and Ragazzino attended a Team Semper Fi event in Washington, D.C. Hurricane Sandy hit the coast during the time they were due to fly back to California, and all flights were canceled. A mandatory lockdown was declared for two days in the hotel where they were staying. Tyler and Ragazzino have friends in New York City and were very concerned about their safety during the storm. Once the lockdown was lifted, they rented a car and headed to New York. Their friends were safe. They stayed for a few days assisting with cleanup. Ragazzino expressed to Tyler how she wished she could stay and help longer.

While on their flight back to San Diego, Ragazzino found an ad in the airline's in-flight magazine. It was a sign, she told Michelle. The ad was for The Mission Continues, a nonprofit agency that empowers veterans to become citizen leaders. This interested her. Through The Mission Continues, she knew she would have an opportunity "to get back into life and to give to life." The Mission Continues would give her a goal. She applied in the fall of 2012.

In December 2012, while awaiting approval from The Mission Continues, Ragazzino was asked to return to Soldiers to Summits to be a mentor and go to Ecuador. They asked her to be a mentor because they recognized her growth since the trip to Nepal. She traveled with a new group of veterans, stepping up and feeling pride in herself and in an organization that had changed her life. In the Marine Corps, Ragazzino was a leader, a staff sergeant on the fast track to being a gunny. Now, as a civilian, she was no longer allowing herself to be a victim, to be abused. She was chosen to be a mentor. She wanted to give back.

When she returned from Ecuador, Ragazzino got the news that her application for The Mission Continues internship was approved. She had to choose a nonprofit, and NYC was still on her mind. After researching and reaching out for suggestions, the Injured Marine Semper Fi Fund suggested Friends of Firefighters, a group dedicated to addressing the physical, mental health, and wellness needs of New York City's firefighters and their families. Friends of Firefighters played a strategic role in the Hurricane Sandy cleanup and recovery.

By being an advocate for first responders, Ragazzino has found her life calling. She is opening the door to further awareness and bridging the military and civilian communities. She said it's not much different from being a Marine. "The military and firefighters have a lot in common. Camaraderie. When the alarm goes off, you respond."

Sandy became Ragazzino's Iraq. During the recovery from Hurricane Sandy, she distributed products to the firefighters and their families who had fallen victim to the devastating storm. Through heartbreak, pain, and suffering, she saw resilience and joy, she said. "You really find the human spirit. Houses were gone and there was destruction everywhere, but the human spirit lives."

Helping others has in turn helped Ragazzino heal, but that's not why she volunteers. She volunteers because she wants to continue serving her country. "I was born to serve. I don't understand why I have that calling, but I do. By doing something for others, I feel fulfilled." With a pure heart, Ragazzino embraces her calling.

Volunteering has a way of illuminating the good in people. "When you take yourself out of yourself and your misery and realize you're a gift—learn to love yourself—you can give back tenfold," she said. "You're that gift."

As a retired injured veteran, Ragazzino wanted to give back to the community. She has a travel schedule that civilians might find daunting, but in her world—the veteran world—it's not so crazy. Ragazzino calls California her home but flies to NYC multiple times throughout the year to volunteer. She is grateful for Tyler being with her every step along the way, providing continued support and daily care. She is more than Ragazzino's VA caregiver—she is her family.

In 2013, in the middle of her internship with The Mission Continues, Tyler and Ragazzino went to San Diego to see what services the city had for Ragazzino. Tyler had seen a sign showing that Bob Filner was now the mayor. He had told them two years earlier to come see him if things didn't get resolved or if they needed his assistance. So they did. This time, they were seeking information about housing for vets and city services. Maybe the city could help out with the VA issues as well.

On June 11, 2013, Tyler and Ragazzino met in the mayor's office in City Hall, San Diego. At the end of the meeting, Filner asked Ragazzino and the VA rep to excuse themselves. When the door closed behind them, he sexually harassed Tyler.

Tyler/Ragazzino is one of several lawsuits that have been filed against the City of San Diego for failure to train Filner on sexual harassment. In 2015, their case was still pending.

In 2014, Ragazzino went to a leadership academy called ChoiceCenter Leadership University in Las Vegas, attending on a veteran's study scholarship. The course, which spans a period of one hundred days, teaches participants how to embrace their lives.

Ragazzino went through an emotional intelligence training course, which enabled her to reach a place within herself that needed healing due to trauma and war. Since the training, she has been able to face life experiences that were holding her back. The center gave her the tools she needed to move on. "It's not that they fixed me," she said. "They showed me what was already in me." It was just forgotten along the way. "It's all still there," Ragazzino said. "The trauma is still there, but the way I think about it has changed. I see the light at the end of the tunnel."

"You can be a victim or survivor, or choose to thrive," Ragazzino said. "I choose to thrive, and I want to be able to show others that they possess the ability to do that as well."

In May 2015, Sen. Marty Golden inducted Ragazzino into the New York State Senate Veterans' Hall of Fame in Albany. "Katherine is most deserving of this special recognition, which is a testament to her courage and sacrifice as shown through her commitment to the United States Marines and the New York City Firefighter," Golden stated. "It is an honor to have inducted

Katherine into the State Senate Veterans' Hall of Fame so that throughout our great State, folks can learn and be inspired by the story of her life. She is truly a hero, and this generation and those that follow will do well in learning of her story of patriotism and service."

On Being Authentic
Commander Vicki Hudson

VICKI HUDSON FACED MANY BATTLES IN HER THIRTY-THREE-YEAR Army career. Some battles were expected, the norm, but it was those in her personal life that have given her some of the greatest satisfaction.

As far back as she can remember, Hudson knew what she wanted to be when she grew up. At age twelve, she told a teacher that she was going to be a soldier. During her childhood, she listened to the stories of her ancestors, which she traces all the way back to the American Revolution. She felt responsible at a young age to give back to this country.

Her parents were teachers and traveled a lot. While in Europe when she was seventeen, she saw what was available or unavailable in other countries. This gave Hudson an early appreciation for what America had to offer and worked to reinforce her patriotism.

At seventeen, Hudson wanted to enlist in the Army, but her mother refused to sign the papers. She wanted her daughter to go to college first. Hudson entered college just after her eighteenth birthday and high school graduation in 1977. In 1979, she entered Army ROTC. She left school the following year, but because she was contracted in ROTC she was required to remain in the reserves. She entered the service in 1979 and spent five years in active and reserve enlisted service to attain the rank of corporal.

In 1984, she returned to the University of Central Florida, enrolled in the ROTC, and upon graduation was commissioned a second lieutenant in the military police corps. This commission marked the transition from enlisted to officer in Hudson's Army career. Hudson served as a noncommissioned officer and commissioned officer in the military police corps, and also as a civil affairs and information operations officer. While a lieutenant, she deployed to Saudi Arabia with the 351st Military Police Company, 160th Military Police Battalion (Combat Support), in support of Operations Desert Shield and Storm, the first of five career deployments.

After Desert Storm, she was promoted to captain and assigned to the Individual Mobilization Augmentee (IMA) program. She was trained and certified as an Army instructor and small-group leader for the United States Army Military Police School. She held this position for two years until her second deployment, this time with the 411th Civil Affairs Battalion for the first rotation of soldiers into Bosnia-Herzegovina in 1996.

Captain Hudson was promoted to major in 2000. Immediately following the September 11 attacks, she was assigned as an IMA with the 16th Military Police Brigade, Fort Bragg, North Carolina. She led an infrastructure security assessment team (ISAT) for the United States Army Corps of Engineers, assessing critical civilian infrastructure with significant economic national interest.

Following her six-month ISAT tour and five months inactive status, Hudson was mobilized for one year as a joint antiterrorism officer with the Force Protection Directorate of the United States

Transportation Command; she oversaw force protection requirements and assessments for all Transportation Command assets,
including transport operations in and out of Afghanistan and
Iraq and prisoner transport for Guantanamo Bay, Cuba.

In 2004, while enrolled in the Defense Information School
for her public affairs officer qualification, she transferred to a
critical-need civil affairs unit preparing to deploy to Iraq, where
she assumed command of Alpha Company, 425th Civil Affairs
Battalion, Santa Barbara, California. Under her command,
Alpha Company went from 3 percent to 97 percent strength.
In ten months, Hudson trained and prepared the unit for
deployment, and it mobilized in April 2005 for deployment to
Iraq. During mobilization, she was transferred to the 401st Civil
Affairs Battalion.

In Iraq, she was detailed to the government transition team,
working directly with provincial elected officials in education,
women's economic development, and law enforcement. As a
field-grade officer, she also participated in a weekly guard duty
shift since the unit was small yet responsible for a corner of the
perimeter. She also volunteered for and was assigned battalion
security convoy team leader, commanding approximately nineteen convoys during her time with the 401st.

After her return from Iraq, Hudson was selected for promotion to lieutenant colonel and promoted upon assignment as
the Operations officer (G3), 4th Brigade, for the 104th Training
Division, Camp Parks, California, in September 2006. In September 2009, she became the G3 on the commanding general's staff
of the 11th Military Police Brigade. In May 2010, Hudson was
reassigned to temporary command of the 2nd Battalion, 95th
Regiment Military Police, an MP training battalion.

In September 2010, she was board-selected to command the
724th Military Police Battalion. In February 2012, Lieutenant

Colonel Hudson relinquished command upon receipt of a mission to prepare for deployment to Afghanistan with another battalion. When this mission was scrubbed, she returned home from Fort Bliss and accepted command of the 304th Information Operations Battalion, 152nd Information Operations Group, Camp Parks, California. In this role—her final command and military assignment—Hudson transformed a newly activated unit into an operationally ready unit that was supporting global operations before it was even one year from activation.

All three of the battalions Hudson commanded had performance issues. "Each battalion when I took command was at the bottom of its brigade, red-lined across all metrics. My job was to get the metrics green and the soldiers ready for war," she said. "The commander is accountable for all training, but it's the NCOs who implement the training and who are supposed to enforce standards set by the Army and the commander. The most senior NCOs in each battalion liked doing things their way, which often left soldiers performing at substandard levels," Hudson said. When she left command, each battalion had risen from the bottom to within reach of the top rankings. But getting the low performers up to standard meant having to interact with some who were used to just getting by and didn't like being called to task.

As you can see, Hudson prepared for and met a number of challenges in her military career. But perhaps her greatest battle has been the one of authenticity. That started when she realized she was a lesbian and came out first in her personal life, and then later as a professional soldier. When she went to college, Hudson didn't even know what the word "lesbian" meant. Once she realized she was lesbian, her coming out was about self-identification and not just sexual orientation. She felt most comfortable within the lesbian community. First, Hudson came out in her personal life. If she had come out in her professional life at that time, there would have been significant consequences under pre–"Don't Ask, Don't Tell" (DADT) regulations against gays in the military and under DADT itself. That would have been "professional suicide." DADT would not end until 2011.

Because of DADT, Hudson had to live a lie. This became a greater challenge when she began to date Monika, who would eventually become her wife and the mother of their two children. Monika, a psychologist, and Hudson started dating seven months before the attacks on September 11, 2001. Over the next five years, Hudson was recalled to active duty three times as a military police or civil affairs officer, including her tour in 2005 to Iraq. Hudson's extensive mobilized active duty and travel on temporary duties for the Army, either as a battalion commander or brigade operations officer, meant that she and Monika endured many months with their relationship invisible and left Monika without any support. The most excruciating times were when Hudson was in Iraq, leading convoys. If something had happened to her in Iraq, Hudson explained, Monika wouldn't have been contacted. Instead, a family member with whom she was estranged would have been notified as her next of kin, in keeping with requirements to list family only on notification documents. It didn't make sense.

Also, when they began dating, Monika was very open about her sexual orientation. She would have to reenter the closet in some ways as the relationship became more serious. This left Monika with no military family support because of existing policies, but also with limited or no community support. She was the hidden military spouse and the closeted lesbian, separated from the LGBT community at home because of military secrecy. It was double isolation for her.

In Mosul in 2005, Hudson's mission in civil affairs was to help the local Iraqis improve women's roles in their society, coach the provincial government on developing a democratically based government public education program, and improve civil rights. She met with provincial elected representatives and worked with them on developing civil projects. For instance, the public educational system was corrupt, the legal system was rife with abuse, and women were significantly marginalized. The government was not accountable to its citizens. In a sense, the U.S. Army had to teach the value of bureaucracy, an odd role for Hudson, who is somewhat of a maverick in other aspects of her life. During daily update briefings, the commanding general would remind her and the other soldiers not to tell the Iraqis what to do. Instead, the mission was to ask them what they wanted and to coach the Iraqis on employing democratic principles for political and social leadership.

While in Mosul, Hudson developed a friendship with an Iraqi woman named Nadia, whom she worked with developing women's economic growth. Nadia was a mother, about fifty years old, who singlehandedly reformed the way prisoners were treated and also pursued improved opportunities for women's economic development. One of the general officers Hudson worked for used to say that if there were ever going to be a woman president of Iraq, Nadia would be that leader. A few months after Hudson left Iraq, Nadia was ambushed and assassinated when leaving Camp Courage, the U.S. base in Mosul.

Hudson commanded nineteen convoys, volunteering for convoy duty while every other officer in the battalion refused convoy command and all but one refused assignment to the convoy team. When asked years later about the risk of leading convoys, Hudson simply stated, "We were lucky. Everyone came home."

After the war, the healing that Hudson needed presented itself physically and emotionally, neither of which is easily identifiable or fixable. Physically, during the 1991 Gulf War, Hudson injured her knee while responding to a chemical alarm. She also has Gulf War illness (or chronic multisymptom illness, as the VA terms it), an assortment of medically unexplained chronic symptoms that can include headaches, joint pain, fatigue, insomnia, dizziness, indigestion, respiratory disorders, and memory problems. She attributes the disease to her having been exposed to chemical weapons (there was a positive detection on her perimeter in Iraq), pesticide-impregnated uniforms, and nerve agent medication. It seems everyone got the same dose, whether a 230-pound male or a 125-pound woman. Additionally, both in the first Gulf War in 1991 and in Mosul in 2005, her living areas regularly were enveloped with the smoke from burn pits in the mornings and evenings. The smoke and other toxic air exposures in both wars contributed to chronic bronchitis and chronic obstructive pulmonary disease (COPD). The extent of burn pit–related illness remains unknown, although the VA does now maintain a database for burn pit exposure.

Hudson also had to deal with sexual harassment and gender discrimination throughout her career. She was perceived to be a lesbian—not because of her behavior, but because she didn't fit in as a strong, aggressive female leader. She entered the Army as part of the first generation of women after the end of the Women's Army Corps in 1978, and while women spread throughout the ranks in all but combat positions, the culture didn't keep up. Even twelve years later, in the first Gulf War, women encountered harassment, discrimination, chronic disregard, and hostility. As a result, Hudson isolated herself within her units and often confronted others or intervened when harassment or discrimination occurred due to race or gender. This isolation was compounded by the hidden life she was forced to lead as a lesbian in the military.

For thirty years, she's had to internalize who she was. Because she was a reservist, Hudson didn't live in military communities. Instead, she often lived far away from military bases. The distance reduced the threat of the military discovering her identity. She accepted assignments in units that were hours or a plane ride away from home so as not to run into soldiers from the unit in the local community. However, these distant assignments didn't prevent her from feeling she needed to lead two separate lives.

She had two different phones and lines for her work and personal life. She took the same precautions with her e-mail addresses. Hudson couldn't bring other soldiers over to her house; all of her relationships were therefore stilted. No one knew who she was or anything about her family. This made her seem unapproachable and untrustworthy in a culture where you must depend upon the person next to you.

Hudson survived two "witch hunts" during her service and was one of the first clients of Servicemembers Legal Defense Network (SLDN) when it was founded in 1993. In September 2010, Monika was part of a small group of LGBT military spouses who met with DoD General Counsel Jeh Johnson, Gen. Carter Ham, and the Pentagon Comprehensive Review Working Group to share stories about the experience of being a hidden, invisible military spouse. This was an important contribution toward the repeal that came a year later of the "Don't Ask, Don't Tell" Policy. On September 20, 2011, when DADT officially ended, Hudson came out as a gay U.S. soldier. She was the commander of the 724th Military Police Battalion at the time. As a leader, Hudson didn't feel as though she had a choice of whether or not to come out. "If I continued to remain hidden, I would be telling my soldiers that it wasn't safe," she said. As far as she knows, she's one of the first battalion commanders across the United States military to come out immediately following the repeal of DADT.

How did she come out? Hudson started at the unit level by putting family photos on her desk. She shared stories about her wife when her first sergeant told stories about his. In the battalion, it was a subtle action. However, she also had to tell her brigade commander, who had presented homophobic with his frequent comments prior to the repeal regarding gays not belonging in the military. She'd now been asked to take part in a civil suit against the military regarding recognition of spouses of gay and lesbian servicemembers and had to tell her boss.

For some time, she'd had to listen to his critical comments about gays and lesbians and how they didn't belong in the military. Now she had to let him know that one of his battalion commanders was a lesbian. That didn't go well. "A week before I brought up the subject of the lawsuit and my part in it, we'd had the usual officer-and-supervisor phone call, where we discussed issues and performance. He told me I was doing well, no issues. A week after I told him I was a lesbian and about the lawsuit, we had another check-in. Now I was 'the worst commander in the brigade and shouldn't be a colonel.' Yeah, there was an impact," Hudson said.

As a soldier, Hudson earned many ribbons, medals, and awards, but it's what she has done more recently that has presented her with the greatest personal satisfaction and brought her some healing. In October 2011, Hudson and her wife, Monika, with SLDN, challenged the constitutionality of the Defense of Marriage Act (DOMA) via landmark litigation (*McLaughlin v. Panetta*). DOMA stated that federal law would only recognize marriage between a man and a woman as a legal union in the United States. Because of current laws, the DoD could not extend recognition or benefits to gay and lesbian military families. In taking part in the lawsuit, Hudson and Monika wanted to make the military a safer place for all families. Despite the potential landmine effect on Hudson's career, she and Monika felt strongly that standing up for gay and lesbian families and fighting an unjust and unequal law was the right action to take. As an officer sworn to uphold the Constitution and bound by the ethos of duty, honor, and country, Hudson saw no other option but to take part in the suit against her employer, the United States of America.

The following year, Hudson, Monika, and other plaintiffs received the Barry Winchell Courage Award for challenging DOMA. On October 2, 2013, a judgment was filed putting into law that same-sex military and veteran spouses were entitled to benefits. The judgment followed the successful U.S. Supreme Court challenge of Edith Windsor, whose case before the court resulted in DOMA being ruled as unconstitutional. This successfully changed the definition of "spouse" in Title 10, 32, and 38 of U.S. Code. The president also directed the executive branch to cease enforcement of sections that limited veterans benefits only to opposite-sex couples. The Department of Veteran Affairs is working to implement this directive.

Hudson was asked to take this stand for equality of access for military families that are gay/lesbian and for gay/lesbian spouses to be fully recognized. She accepted the challenge and the public sacrifice to take part in litigation against her employer. She is proud that her family's story is contained in a brief submitted in the Windsor case and that it was one of the many stories told in arguments before the Supreme Court.

These lawsuits weren't easy. If anything, they created more exposure and vulnerabilities. But when Hudson was asked to be part of the lawsuit, she didn't feel as though she had a choice. Statistics indicated there were gay and lesbian soldiers in her command. Hudson believed one in ten of the population were gay, a commonly accepted number based upon Alfred Kinsey's research, and thus there would be other gay and lesbian soldiers in her formations. Gallup polls in recent years have shown a range of estimates, some as high as 25 percent of the population. The 2013 National Health Survey indicated a smaller number, approximately 3 percent of the population. Hudson took part in the lawsuit as a commander responsible for the health and welfare of her unit; otherwise, her family and her soldiers' families wouldn't be cared for because as far as the Army was concerned, their families did not exist. This violated her sense of integrity and what she saw as her duty as an officer and commander: "the hard right over the easy wrong. What's right isn't always career-enhancing," she said.

As a commander, Hudson was a role model. If she didn't take action by coming out, she believed she would be betraying her soldiers and the trust that is implicit between leader and the led. By coming out and standing up for her rights, Hudson was helping her gay and lesbian soldiers live normal lives. "Those of us who came out early paved the way for those who came out later," Hudson said. "I lived two lives, never being part of either world. Everyone should be able to live an authentic life."

When she left the 724th MP Battalion, Hudson received a card from one of the soldiers, thanking her for coming out. That soldier wasn't yet comfortable coming out, but felt better about his own identity as a soldier. That meant the action she and her wife had taken mattered and had made a difference. During Hudson's tenure at the 304th IO Battalion, soldiers from within and outside her command went to see her. They wanted to talk to her about their own process in coming out. But the greatest sense of validation for what she'd done came when the commandant of the NCO Academy, who had been her

G3 command sergeant major when she was the G3 at the 11th MP BDE, pre–DADT repeal, told her that his service with her before the repeal, and knowing her after, had helped him with soldiers at the NCO Academy who had struggles coming out in the service. That was validating.

She's still discovering how to heal. Writing helps. It's healing because it takes Hudson on a journey and she comes into contact with what's buried deep inside. She never knows where the journey is going to take her. She has a master's degree in creative nonfiction writing and writes poetry along with prose. She's done some work in the women's veterans community and was active as an officer in a Veterans of Foreign Wars (VFW) post for a while.

She's still adjusting to being out of the Army. She retired in December 2012. As a "gray area" retiree, it's like being in military retiree purgatory, she said. There is no retiree pension and no access to any retiree assistance programs, as one is not viewed as a true retiree until after age sixty, when reserve retirement pensions begin disbursement. In a way, the "gray area creates another category of invisibility," Hudson said.

Hudson is looking deeper into what needs to be healed. She's more aware of her feelings, which had become numb, a classic PTSD symptom. She's had to relearn how to feel emotions again because for a long time she had only two: anger and neutrality.

Making connections with others is also healing but not one of her strengths. Hudson's an introvert who finds it draining to be around too many people. She belongs to veterans groups (VFW and Disabled American Veterans) but doesn't really participate. She has reconnected with the rugby community by becoming a youth and collegiate coach, and she is the training officer for her local referee society. Recently, she has been working with her local congressional representative's office to address access to retirement benefits for "gray area" reserve/

guard retirees who are also at least 70 percent disabled veterans, something currently not allowed by law. In general, though, she still tends toward isolation.

While in the service, people didn't say derogatory things to her face once she reached field grade. "Women leaders tolerate a lot more disrespect than men on a daily basis, particularly at company grade," Hudson said. "As a woman, you can't fight every battle that comes up. I think the women in the military who aren't perceived as lesbians, which incidentally often has nothing to do with their actual sexual orientation, who present more traditionally feminine, are more accepted and less challenged."

Early in her career, Hudson was often the only woman in some of the small units she was assigned to, or one of a handful of women in the company, who worked hard at soldiering and didn't use gender as a way to skate by. She endured negative comments, sexual innuendos, and unwanted sexual invitations—sexual harassment—from superiors. In the first Gulf War, Hudson's direct supervisor asked her daily for sex. An officer from another unit whom she briefed daily on force protection made a pass. The battalion field grades—the commander, executive officer, and S3—were harassing the pretty blonde young specialist (E4), and a couple times Hudson had to physically put herself between the soldier and the major. She was a first lieutenant at the time.

The S3 solicited erotic letters from some of the women, and when he got to Hudson, she was the only one who refused. She was harangued daily about the letter. She reported sexually based hazing in the unit and received death threats as a result—in a combat zone, where everyone had their own guns and bullets. She was belittled and humiliated daily, and her authority as an officer was often challenged because of others' disregard for a woman officer. As she rose through the ranks, the disregard often remained, but the acting out became much more subtle.

She never had problems with younger soldiers and leaders. It was the older soldiers who were more entrenched in their beliefs and the old Army culture where women were not accepted.

"It was interesting that in every unit I've ever commanded that went to war soon after I left, soldiers have reached out to tell me how the tough standards I'd set and enforced resulted in their being able to better perform under the strain of a combat zone. How they felt I'd made a difference in making sure they came home. And in each one, it was the senior NCOs who fought me every step of the way," Hudson said.

Hudson was a commander of three battalions where the leaders failed to do their jobs. Often she was the only senior ranked woman and, once DADT was repealed, the only "out" soldier in her unit. Certainly she was going to feel an impact. But the pathway is open now for women and lesbians. There are many female senior leaders, and some of them are lesbians.

"Many women will not experience the discrimination and gender harassment that I, and others, experienced," Hudson said. "With the recent openings of combat assignment jobs for women, this will only get better as women demonstrate they can fulfill the essence of what it means to be a soldier—to seek out and close with the enemy. I think the recent graduation of three women from the Army's Ranger School demonstrates this: both that women are capable and that the culture is changing. I won't be part of the next generation of the integrating of the force for all, but I'm proud I was able to help pave the way for others, or widen the road from what those before me had already done."

These days, Hudson is a stay-at-home mom. She coaches rugby, volunteers on veterans issues, and, when not writing, plays a little World of Warcraft. She resides in Hayward, California, with her wife and their two children. She is a freelance writer and published author. Each year, she sponsors a contest for emerging writers that awards the winner with registration to the San Francisco Writers Conference. She is also fundraising for a scholarship for veterans in creative writing at her alma mater, St. Mary's College of California.

An Advocate for the Ages

Pvt. Kate Weber

Today she advocates for rape victims. It would take her fifteen years after her own rape before she could actually speak out about it. But since she started talking, she hasn't stopped.

From Marin County, California, to Capitol Hill, Kate Weber has made her story known. She's become so good at telling her story that in 2013 she was named Woman Veteran Leader of the Year by the Department of Veterans Affairs in California, a state with more than a million veterans. Today she displays the leadership formed by who she was and what she has gone through over the past twenty years.

Weber joined the Army in 1993 at the age of seventeen. She went through training and shipped off to Fürth, Germany, for her first duty station as a transportation management coordinator. Her job was to move military shipments across Germany using the German railroad.

She had been there less than two weeks but still hadn't received a paycheck, so she went to the finance officer to see what was going on. He turned out to be a sergeant from her original hometown in Illinois (her family had moved to the Bay Area in California when she was five). Being so far from home, Weber felt like she had made a friend.

Later that evening, Weber went out with a group of soldiers to a civilian dance club. The finance sergeant was there. Earlier in the day he had issued Weber a check for $1,000. He obviously had some authority and had been generous to her. During the course of the evening, the sergeant approached Weber. Beside him was his pregnant wife. He said something like, "Hey, private, next time you take a smoke break, come and get me. I need to talk to you about your paycheck." So when the time came, Weber got the sergeant and they walked outside together. There were no red flags.

She followed him to the second story of a fire escape, where she thought they would sit, smoke, and talk. Instead, he raped her, punched her in the face, and threw her off the second-floor balcony. It wasn't until she awoke on the street that Weber realized she was naked from the waist down. She got up, pulled her shirt and skirt down from her torso, and fled to a taxi. She was in shock. The sergeant was two completely different men—one the man in the finance office, the other a violent rapist.

She was terrified. "I dissociated immediately," recalled Weber, who has spent nearly twenty years in therapy since that night. "My experience with the rape was more from outside my body. I feel like I was watching what was happening to me from above." Dissociating is a coping skill our bodies use to endure trauma. "It was a gift to be able to dissociate at the time," she said.

Because the Army was in the process of closing its base there, Fürth was nearly a ghost town. There were no MPs and no police response to her rape. Weber went to the hospital and told the lieutenant colonel on duty that she had been raped by a sergeant. She complained of cervical pain, but no rape kit was done. She was never examined by a doctor. Instead, she was given Vicodin for the pain along with a note that said she had been sexually assaulted.

When she got home from the ER, the rapist was waiting in her room. He held her by the throat and threatened her. She had better get an AIDS test to prove to him that she didn't have AIDS from living in the Bay Area and that she hadn't given it to him and to his pregnant wife, whom he'd had sex with after he raped Weber.

"He had no fear because he knew he wasn't going to get into trouble," Weber said. "Nobody gave a shit about me." She was labeled the unit's whore, and other soldiers were told to beware or else she'd claim they raped her. "I've never been that girl and am not that girl now."

Before she traveled from the United States to Germany, Weber, like all soldiers, had a medical checkup to make sure she wasn't pregnant and didn't have HIV or any sexually transmitted diseases. Weber promised her attacker she wouldn't say anything. And two weeks after she arrived in Germany, she was retested for HIV, STDs, and pregnancy. She kept the written results in the side pocket of her uniform, and every day she waited to run into the rapist so she could give him the test results. Eventually he came to her room. She gave him the papers, and he never bothered her again. A month later she moved into another barracks.

No one believed Weber. No one questioned the sergeant. No one cared, obviously. "I had his semen in me and no one did a rape test" at the emergency room, she said. "They didn't know as much about rape or about female soldiers in the early 1990s as they do now." According to the *New York Daily News,* as late as 2011, "the Pentagon argued in civilian court that rape and sexual assault are just 'occupational hazards' of joining the military."

Weber was never so physically fit, stable, spiritually sound, and solid a human being as she was in the days leading up to the rape. She had just graduated from boot camp and training and was ready to make a career out of the Army. "If someone had helicoptered me 20 miles out into the ocean and told me to find my way back, I would have," she said. "I was convinced that I was a survivor."

From the back porch of her home in Rohnert Park, California, Weber recounted the past two decades. She shed a tear or two and took some hits of her medicinal marijuana. Remembering that time still pulls forth a huge amount of anxiety and grief.

After the rape, Weber started to doubt herself—doubts that proved to be dangerous. She began ignoring any and all red flags. She stopped trusting her gut, her instincts. This led to fifteen more years of trauma. She thought there was something wrong with her alert system. Her instincts never told her that the sergeant was going to rape her. So after feeling that her instincts had betrayed her, she didn't think she could trust her own intuitions again. It messed up her life. She made a series of wrong decisions, including spouses: Weber has been married three times. "I just submitted," she said.

She was always low-key, but following the rape she started to sleep around a little and became mean and controlling. "I lost my mind," she said. "These weren't intimate, loving relationships. I just wanted to fuck someone's head up." She kicked a guy out of her house when he failed to get an erection. She spent so much time trying to fake it that she became hardened. She wanted to get her power back but didn't know how. She wasn't covering up her personal issues very well and was told she was about to get kicked out of the Army.

Nine months after she arrived in Germany, Weber was honorably discharged. During the rape, when she was thrown off the two-story fire escape, she'd suffered several blown discs. She never saw an orthopedist in Germany. She was in pain, and it grew to be severe. She gained 20 pounds. Instead of being discharged for being raped and thrown off a building, she was discharged for weight-control failure. She lost the GI Bill because soldiers have to be in the service for twenty-four months, and she had only been in for twenty.

Three days after her discharge, Weber was on her mother's couch—homeless, jobless, and feeling worthless. And because the man who raped her was black with green eyes, now she thought every black man with green eyes was a rapist. This was a change for someone living in the Bay Area who didn't have a racist bone in her body.

The rape changed how she viewed everything, including her home and work lives. When she was twenty-three, she couldn't wait to get married, become a housewife, and hide in her home. She didn't want to work anymore. Over the years she filed for disability for PTSD and MST in 2003. At the age of twenty-nine, she was declared permanently and totally disabled.

She went to the VA for fifteen years before she started healing. She doesn't blame the VA. "I was faking it," she said. "They weren't purging the trauma. They were just counseling me. I'd tell the doc what I was doing, what happened the past week, and the discomfort." Nothing seemed to be helping except pills like Zoloft.

Then she started taking pain pills. These gave her anxiety, so she began taking antianxiety pills. Soon she had a basketful of pills, not unlike the mounting pile of drugs other veterans have been prescribed. Because the talk therapy wasn't working, Weber began abusing her medication. To make matters worse, in 2006 she was diagnosed with melanoma, while she was still breast-feeding her son. Getting cancer "reiterated the idea that I'm not supposed to be here," she said. "I'm going to die young."

First she was raped. Then addicted to pills. Now she had cancer. What next? What must a person endure in her lifetime? Surely the other shoe was going to drop. And she knew she couldn't tolerate one more thing. She used cancer as an excuse to increase her pain medication for her back. She had worked with a pain clinic and gone from taking Vicodin to methadone. That changed everything. The methadone caused her so much anxiety that she started taking antianxiety medications such as Klonopin and Valium.

At thirty-nine, she had the maturity level of a twenty-one-year-old. She believes her emotional growth was slowed by her rape. "I notice that in peer groups and relationships I'm different," she said. "Sometimes my PTSD has made it really hard for me to have girlfriends and relationships with women because I was so severely traumatized and didn't know it."

From 1994, when she was raped, until 2009, Weber had no coping skills. In 2009, she started the process of learning them. She was the only woman in her support group at the VA. The men have become big brothers to her.

In 2009, she also realized she wasn't going to die from the cancer. But she might die soon of something else. She was drooling on herself and behaving like a zombie. She couldn't balance anything. She'd spend three to four days in her bathrobe. "I was killing myself with the pills," she said. "If I wasn't able to do that, I would have committed suicide." She believes she was suicidal for fifteen years, from the rape to the present. She knows how she would have killed herself: by overdose. But she could never get her kids out of her mind. There's no way she could do it.

Weber has been married three times. The abuse of prescription drugs increased when her son's father, an Army recruiter, left. Weber gave birth to Ryan without her parents or family around. Her husband had isolated her from her family over the years and then moved into a girlfriend's house while Weber was in the hospital delivering Ryan.

When Ryan was six months old, Weber met Troy on a blind date through a mutual friend. Weber and Troy are now married, and Troy has been Kate's number one supporter and a great co-parent. Troy has a son and daughter, TJ and Taylor, from a previous marriage. Kate also has a daughter, Morgan, from her second previous marriage.

"They [Troy and her children] are the reason I'm here and why I'm not going anywhere," she said. Ryan, her youngest, is in special education. She knows God would not have chosen her to have a child with special needs unless He thought she could handle it. Now, she and her son go through their healing together. Sometimes he'll ask her eight times a day if she loves him because he was abandoned by his dad.

When she believed she was probably going to die from the pills, Weber decided to go off everything cold turkey. She went to a residential women's trauma, drug, and alcohol rehab program. During fourteen days as an inpatient, Weber had at least one seizure and was admitted to the emergency room. There was no way she could have gotten off the drugs by herself. The pain was unbelievable. She was up all night long. The staff wouldn't give her anything to help her sleep. She wrote in her journal that she thought she was dying. Reading what she had written made her realize how severely she had been medicating herself.

In the program, Weber started to attend Narcotics Anonymous. She began working the twelve steps and forgave herself. Narcotics Anonymous got her clean and sober. Since then, being an advocate for women like herself—women who have been raped in the military—has kept her alive. She gave up on the civilian inpatient program, but not on her recovery. Her husband picked her up, and on the way home, Weber began to recognize the definition in the trees and the different shades of green. She had depth perception for the first time in years. In the past, everything had blended together. Now she was on a pink cloud, talking about how great life was sober. Several years later, she is still on that cloud. She continues to think life is awesome and that she has so many things to be grateful for.

For fourteen months she went to an Narcotics Anonymous/Alcoholics Anonymous meeting every day, but she felt no sense of obligation to anyone to attend. She did have commitments at three to four meetings a week. The bad news was that her family didn't see much of her. The good news was that NA was keeping her going. It was working.

Then she got an incredible offer. Weber was chosen to be in the movie *The Invisible War*, about men and women who had been raped in the military. Her role in the movie was followed up with an invitation to participate in the Artemis Recovery Program in Santa Barbara on a ranch owned by Ted Turner and Jane Fonda. This program for MST survivors is now located at Boulder Crest Retreat in Virginia and continues to help veterans with MST for free.

Artemis offered her a spiritual awakening through somatic and gestalt therapies and through many other services the program provided. Somatic therapy is a physical way to work out trauma. As part of gestalt therapy, Weber put a picture of her dad across from her and had conversations with him.

The program had a top-notch chef who prepared quality food for participants. Part of the healing process involved Weber spending time with the chef. She rolled up her sleeves and used a mortar and pestle to make pesto. She was learning how to become a participant in her own life. She realized that cooking aromas such as garlic were therapeutic for her. These days, she knows if she needs to get grounded or centered, one way to do that is by getting some garlic and cooking. The scent of lavender also has a calming effect on her.

At Artemis, one of Weber's epiphanies was realizing she had ignored the red flags in her life. It all made sense. She began to forgive herself for missing those flags. At the top of the mountain there was a hot tub. "Every morning, afternoon, and evening, I was in Jane Fonda's hot tub, looking out over the ocean and reading happy books," Weber said. "I didn't have any pain up there. I could feel my body healing in the water."

She was eating healthy foods and no longer smoking cigarettes or weed, or drinking. She was learning how to be inside her body again. Weber was also learning what helps her heal. When she started getting sober she tried massage, which helped her feel comfortable in her body. Acupuncture reduces her tension.

Weber left "an emotional rucksack" of previously unprocessed trauma at the Artemis program, she said. Her inner forgiveness—self-forgiveness—has handed her permission to be okay with the things she likes about herself and to share these with others. When she first got her VA money, she felt capable of working a job, but that didn't last long. Over time, it became apparent that she could not predict day-to-day abilities. Ten years later, it is evident there is no getting fixed. But there is "a recovery journey with my name on it," she said.

She begged the VA to cover massage and acupuncture. She's working with the VA to show them what kinds of holistic therapies work for her. Unfortunately, it is very difficult to find practitioners outside the VA who are willing to deal with the VA bureaucracy in order to get paid. Many times, veterans must front the cost of therapy themselves and seek reimbursement afterward. If the VA loses your paperwork or claim, the balance due often ends up on the veteran's credit report.

Over the years, Weber has learned she'd rather be an advocate and a leader than a peer supporter working on-on-one with the veteran. After letting women stay at her house who then stole from her, she learned from her VA counselor how to develop boundaries to ensure not only her safety but also her family's. She has chosen to push away some female veterans who have stolen from her or otherwise taken advantage of her, in favor of talking to military leadership and having an open, transparent conversation about the climate and culture women have been forced to serve in—a culture that doesn't serve the purpose of the nation.

Weber began making speaking engagements for Protect Our Defenders, a survivor support network. The nonprofit's mission is to "honor, support and give voice to the brave women and men in uniform who have been raped or sexually assaulted by fellow service members. We seek to fix the military training, investigation and adjudication systems related to sexual violence and harassment—systems that often re-victimize assault survivors by blaming them while failing to prosecute the perpetrators."

Protect our Defenders has given Weber access to legislators whom she never knew she had access to before. For instance, Congresswoman Jackie Speier, who represents San Mateo, met Weber before the launch of Protect Our Defenders. After that, Speier began inviting Weber to numerous functions. Speier has taken Weber to the White House and Capitol Hill. Weber has been back every year since her first visit in 2010.

Weber went to D.C. to introduce Protect Our Defenders to the world at the urging of Panayiota Bertzikis, a Coast Guard veteran who founded the Military Rape Crisis Center (MRCC), which provides free counseling and advice to victims of sexual assault. The goal of MRCC is to talk to the survivor and then find someone in their chain of command who will help them with whatever they need. This occurred after Bertzikis was sexually assaulted. Following her discharge, Bertzikis was awarded the Unsung Heroines of Massachusetts award by the Massachusetts Commission on the Status of Women in May 2010.

Advocating for veterans has been instructive. Weber has singlehandedly changed politicians' minds about the Military Justice Improvement Act and why rape accusations should be taken out of the chain of command. After Weber spent a tireless day in Washington speaking to staff members and senators in November 2014, Sen. Cory Booker of New Jersey went from one senator's office to another in support of the act. Booker tweeted that he was voting for the act. Weber got the tweet when she was in a hotel room by herself. She shared the news with her Facebook group, "Women Veterans for Equality in Our VA System," and got the support she needed.

The Military Justice Improvement Act, which has still not become law, was introduced by Sen. Kirsten Gillibrand of New York, who has worked hard to get it passed but twice has been blocked by the Senate. In June 2015 she got two more votes but not enough to block a filibuster.

When Weber speaks to active-duty personnel, she lets them know about MRCC. The first time I talked to Weber, she was between phone calls with an Army major from Marin County. The major had MST herself, and also had a soldier with MST. The major didn't know what to do for herself, never mind her soldier. MRCC exists for active-duty servicemembers who don't feel they have support on base. "It's active duty helping others get through shitty situations because they have experience," Weber said.

One thing that really made a difference in Weber's healing was meeting with other survivors, a process that requires listening and speaking skills. Weber had been doing the listening with her peer support. Now it was time to speak out.

It all clicked. "For some reason, at thirty-nine the world is ready to listen to me," Weber said. "And I realized I still had a story to tell." In addition to speaking out, she started "MST Recovery Network" on Facebook. It is a private page with about eighty members, each an MST survivor.

Weber continues to be one of the only MST survivors in northern California who speaks up. She hopes her outspokenness will encourage others to step forward and take the microphone. Advocacy has been an effective way for Weber to tell her story. "I couldn't sit by and keep watching it [rape] happen. I didn't have a choice. Now I watch others get stronger. I am watching our military get educated about bystander intervention [a violence-prevention strategy] and it fires me up." Weber is doing advocacy for both veterans and those serving now.

As she advocates, Weber lets her audience know that healing never ends. "Just because I'm in recovery doesn't mean it all goes away," she said. "It's still a part of me. I've had terrible relationships with other people and can't provide for myself the way I would like to."

As part of her recovery, Weber meditates. When she first started to meditate, she was so loaded that she didn't feel anything. There was no shift in energy. She couldn't feel other people's energy, nor could she sense her own. She didn't know or care how others were reading her. She described herself as an "obnoxious bitch." She used to yell at the VA staff, "You owe me. I'm here for rape." Now she sees that attitude in other veterans and it scares her. She doesn't have an ounce of that hostility anymore, she said, although she will still call out the VA when they do something inappropriate. "I feel like I'm the sheriff in town," Weber said. "And they're saying, 'Who are you?' I'm Katie Weber."

She's totally comfortable with who she is now.

A Time to Remember

Chaplain Diana Lantz

"Perhaps you have come to royal dignity for just such a time as this."

—Esther 4:14

THE COBBLER'S CHILDREN ALWAYS GO BAREFOOT.

This saying makes me think of the chaplains in the military. The chaplain looks after the troops, but who ministers to the chaplains? Another chaplain? An enlightened officer? Or do they suffer in silence?

Diana Lantz, a Navy chaplain, was raised in a Christian home in New Zealand. When Lantz was about five or six years old, her Sunday school "prize" for that year was a book about Samuel in the temple. In addition to being involved in church and youth groups, first as a member and then as a leader, she was also part of a Christian parachurch organization called Girls' Brigade. Parachurches, according to Wikipedia, are "Christian faith-based organizations that work outside of and across denominations to engage in social welfare and evangelism, usually independent of church oversight." Through these groups, Lantz earned her Duke of Edinburgh Award, the New Zealand equivalent to the Gold Award in Girl Scouts or the Eagle Scout award in Boy Scouts. She was confirmed at seventeen and ordained a deacon when she was twenty-seven.

Lantz was helping to lead youth group in her late twenties when they had a combined citywide Presbyterian youth group church service one Sunday evening. The minister preached from 1 Samuel, about God calling Samuel in the temple. He concluded his sermon by giving his personal testimony and adding that "some of you could do this," meaning ministry.

"It shot through my head: 'I could,'" Lantz said. "And then I immediately asked myself, 'Where did that come from?'"

"I could," she said after the service to her friend, Bob, a retired Air Force chaplain.

"What?" he asked.

"Do ministry," she said.

"Why don't you?" he said.

"No, I would have to go back to school," she said.

She continued to ignore what she believed was a call to ministry until she visited a couple of friends who had been talking about her. Not knowing about her "call," they gave her the scripture from 1 Corinthians 2:9: "No eye has seen, no ear has heard, no mind has conceived what God has prepared for those who love him."

At that time she was also teaching in a Catholic school, and a song they sang regularly at assembly was "Here I Am, Lord." She took all of these things to be God telling her that she needed to listen to Him and to pray about it. (Years later, at a high school reunion, a classmate told Lantz that her friends had always said she would end up a nun. Lantz had had no idea.)

The first family member she told was her brother, and his response was, "Sure, Di, I always thought you could be like

Leta." The Reverend Leta Hawe was their minister when they were teenagers. She was a pioneer and only the eighth woman to be ordained by the Presbyterian Church in New Zealand. Bob supported her call from the beginning. He committed to supporting Lantz financially while she went through the schooling. Further education was one of the aspects of the call to ministry that she balked at because she couldn't see herself learning Greek and Hebrew. Nevertheless, she surrendered to God and felt the "peace which passeth all understanding," as is written in the Book of Philippians.

After a long courtship with Bob, they got married at the end of 1990. Lantz decided it would be easier for her to move to the States than for him to move to New Zealand, so they got married in New Zealand and she came to America. She was twenty-nine.

At the time of the call, Lantz didn't know what type of ministry she would be involved in. While in seminary she was required to do clinical pastoral education, which she did at Women and Infants Hospital in Providence, Rhode Island. She knew God was calling her to be a chaplain. In the summer of 1995, she was thinking of a hospital chaplaincy.

"I don't know if I can answer exactly what it was that drew me, except to say the variety of people that you meet and the fact that there is seldom a long-term relationship developed," she said. "It's on-the-spot intervention ministry for a brief time. It's a little bit different in the military because the relationships are a little bit longer-term, but there's still always a constant change of people." It's not that she wouldn't like long-term relationships, but in the military you have the mindset of a transient population, Lantz added.

In her second year of seminary, she met a chaplain recruiter. After meeting the recruiter, Lantz thought a career as a military chaplain made sense. The Navy appealed to her because of the variety of duties and opportunities.

Before she got called to the chaplaincy, people would ask Lantz what part of the ministry she would go into, and she would say education, likely because she was coming out of school. It did seem like a natural progression. And yet, when she got to seminary, the two subjects she enjoyed the least were Christian education and ethics.

When Lantz told her mother that she'd been called to the chaplaincy, her mom said she could never see her daughter as a pastor of a parish anyway. But before Lantz could become an active-duty chaplain, she had to be ordained, endorsed by a church, and have her own parish for a couple years.

Toward the end of seminary, Lantz had a conversation with God. "You have to work this out," she said. She knew she wanted to go active duty, but she also had to receive the call to be ordained. Lantz then had to tell a church they were only going to have her for two years because she planned to join the military.

As it happens, God worked it out. Lantz was soon contacted by two small churches in Ohio. She was ordained by Muskingum Valley Presbytery and served as interim pastor for eighteen months at Warsaw and Fresno Presbyterian Churches. At the same time, Bob served two small parishes also located in Coshocton County, Ohio.

She went through chaplain school in the summer of 1998 in Newport, Rhode Island, and was called to active duty in June 1999. Her first tour was Recruit Training Command at Great Lakes, Illinois. To her, that was the best place to start. "Great Lakes was the perfect place for me to start my Navy ministry because I had no prior military experience, and so I 'learned the ropes' from the ground up," she explained. "I became thoroughly familiar with the enlisted experience and have used that knowledge throughout my Navy journey. Also, at that time there were very few civilians on the base, so I learnt from a lot of senior enlisted and Mustangs who were a wealth of knowledge and experience."

She was there for three years, including during 9/11 and the bombing of the USS *Cole*. In the meantime, Bob helped out at a Presbyterian church near Great Lakes and at a small summer church on an island near the Canadian border.

In October 2002, Lantz transferred to the USS *Theodore Roosevelt* aircraft carrier in Norfolk. They weren't supposed to deploy until May 2003, but as so often happens, plans changed. Instead, they were told to pack their sea bags; they may not be coming back. They were deploying with the surge in Iraq in January 2003. They came out of the shipyard before Christmas and were supposed to do a whole workup. After arriving at Vieques Island, near Puerto Rico, in support of training, they hung around the island until they got orders, instead of going back to Norfolk after the training. Then they sailed across the Atlantic to the Mediterranean in support of the war. While Lantz was deployed, Bob was a pastor to the elders at Great Bridge Presbyterian Church in Chesapeake, Virginia.

The war started in March. The USS *Theodore Roosevelt* was stationed northeast of Cyprus, where it circled in the water. There were two carriers: the *Roosevelt*, which did night operations, and the USS *Harry S. Truman*, which did day flights. During shock and awe, planes were launching from the *Roosevelt* and flying into northern Iraq. "It was weird," Lantz said of working nights. "We'd get up at 2200 [10 P.M.] and work 'til 6 in the morning." They did this for five to six weeks and returned to Norfolk in May 2003.

In November 2004, Lantz transferred to the Marines, Combat Logistics Battalion 7 (CLB-7), 1st Marine Logistics Group, in Twentynine Palms, California. They deployed to Iraq in February 2006 and returned in September of that year. So Lantz experienced the war from both sea and land. Shortly after they arrived in California, Bob went to New Zealand to serve as an interim pastor for a small country parish for six months.

As battalion chaplain in Iraq, Lantz was responsible for 1,137 Marines and sailors, including those who worked at the hospital at Al Asad and those in mortuary affairs. She was based at Al Asad Airbase with the majority of her Marines, but her CLB-7 Marines were also attached to Korean Village, Al Qaim, and Haditha Dam. Her Marines served in personnel retrieval and processing, otherwise known as mortuary affairs. There she saw every soldier, sailor, or Marine of Regimental Combat Team 7 that had been killed in action as they passed through the unit's hands.

She also covered the sailors who served in the health services company, otherwise known as the hospital—the next line of care after the battalion corpsman on site had done his job. She saw the joy of men and women who survived and experienced the sorrow of seeing others die.

Lantz befriended a chief warrant officer in mortuary affairs. He experienced PTSD severely after he got home. He was a retired admin officer in the Marine Corps who had gone to work for a funeral home. When the war started, he asked the Marine Corps if it needed someone with his skills. The answer was yes. He worked in TQ and Al Asad, processing thirty to thirty-five soldiers who had been killed in Iraq. When he went home, he fell apart and couldn't go back to his old job. He struggled but is doing better now, Lantz said.

When asked why she needed healing, Lantz, after a long silence, replied, "I often ask myself that question." She's fortunate, she said, because she "doesn't dwell on the crap that we deal with. You can't own it. You help. You do your job. You serve humanity in the name of Christ, but it doesn't become your problem. So I never did that." She doesn't internalize other people's problems. "You can't afford to. Otherwise you'd be a mess."

She certainly had opportunity to dwell on the misfortune of others. When they first arrived, her battalion lost a Marine when a Humvee rolled over. The driver lost control and the gunner was killed. It was their first casualty.

"I wanted to do the best for the battalion and for the family," Lantz said. "My responsibility was the memorial service, which I had to arrange in tandem with the first sergeant."

That casualty was followed by another one. Just before Easter, a convoy took supplies to Haditha, usually a day trip. Lantz didn't go this time, as it left on a Sunday and she had to lead the worship service at Camp Ripper, but she always prayed with the convoy before they departed. A huge thunderstorm erupted during the trip. On their way back from Haditha, the convoy came to a bridge they weren't allowed to cross because of potential IEDs. They always had to ford the wadi, or streambed, instead.

Although usually dry, with the thunderstorm water was under the bridge. The convoy commander and deputy commander elected to cross the water. They sent over a 7-ton truck with a driver and seven people in the back. Halfway across, the force of the water overturned the truck. They lost seven Marines and a sailor in full battle gear. One Marine survived. Seven of the lost belonged to CLB-7. "That was the tragedy that we experienced," Lantz said. It took a week, until Easter morning, for them to find the last Marine.

"I think that's when you go into autopilot," she said. When there was a death, she moved into action. She had a high-profile memorial service to run and a lot of logistics were involved. Generals and colonels would be there. Fortunately for her, "I had an awesome team," she said.

But Lantz is as human as the next person. Autopilot only works for so long. At some point you have to deal with what you've experienced. It always catches up with you. When faced with those moments, she's not above asking God "Why?" when someone dies. And she's not above leaning on Him. She relies heavily on scripture, including one of her favorites, Proverbs 3:5–6: "Trust in the Lord with all your heart, and do not rely on your own insight. In all your ways acknowledge him, and he will make straight your paths."

It's hard for Lantz to know how she was affected by war. For example, she says she did fine. Her definition of "fine" is feeling normal, content, and being able to minister effectively. She had the support network of Marines and sailors she deployed with. Yet she did have a couple of what she called "days of mourning," when she couldn't stop crying. "One time I ended up in the battalion aid station with the corpsmen, just bawling my eyes out and not really knowing why," she said. "The petty officers let me just sit in the back and worked around me until I composed myself and was able to go back to my own office."

Following her tour with the battalion, Lantz got orders for a permanent change of station to the Coast Guard Academy in New London, Connecticut. Bob no longer worked full-time but volunteered at local churches. When Lantz arrived at the academy, her life took a turn for the worse. She was diagnosed with depression and sleep apnea. She's not sure how much of her depression came from PTSD, from the dark night of the soul, or from a midlife crisis. In part, the depression was a result of the sleep apnea. It got better with a CPAP machine that helped her breathe.

Even now there are times when Lantz realizes she is still healing—or doing something that looks like healing. "You don't heal," Lantz said. "You integrate. You don't forget about the experience but integrate it with who you are today." She gets teary-eyed as she recalls Iraq. "There are times when it still hits me."

The triggers are simply remembering and dwelling on the lives lost. "They were Marines, sailors, and soldiers just doing their jobs, but when you look at what the situation is in Iraq now, I can't help but question the worth of their sacrifice," Lantz said.

Other triggers are dates—Easter Sunday especially, or hearing a place like Al Qaim or Al Asad mentioned on the news. Or when she was in Okinawa, meeting Marines again whom she had served with at Al Asad. Especially the first sergeant who had the lead with her on the memorial services and who is now a sergeant major. "It was awesome seeing him again," she said. "It's the 'Band of Brothers' feeling."

As a chaplain, one of the challenges is to help others while you are going through your own stuff. "You have to be careful not to burden someone else with your problems," she said. "You can share with them, but you can't dwell on it in a counseling situation. You can't project your problems onto them." Experience has been Lantz's best teacher. It has taught her what works and doesn't work.

Lantz confided in a squadron chaplain in Iraq. "He was a blessing," she said. "That was God working it out as well." In turn, she was a confidant for a wing chaplain, the highest-ranking chaplain there.

She was lonely during the deployment. There were very few women officers, and she was a sailor in a Marine environment. "Everyone loves the chaplain, but he's always the odd one out," she said. "It was very challenging."

In Iraq, Lantz led Sunday services at Camp Ripper, where Regimental Combat Team 7 was located. Sometimes she felt like the only reason she was in Iraq was to support the regimental colonel. On one occasion, he lost four Marines at one of the forward operating bases. A suicide bomber drove into a sentry post, killing the Marines. The bodies went through Al Asad on their way to Dover. The regimental colonel took the losses personally. He was always in chapel on Sunday morning. Lantz knew that if he wasn't in chapel, something was wrong. She looked after him.

When they lost the four Marines, their engineering company was involved in cleaning up the mess. Lantz was involved in mortuary affairs. The battalion colonel received an e-mail from the regimental colonel, asking him to pass on a word of thanks to those who supported regiment. He especially wanted to thank the chaplain for her support. That was one of the few times someone actually thanked her. A lot of what she and other chaplains do is in confidence and not recognized. For the regimental colonel to single out the chaplain was a big deal, and she appreciated it.

On another occasion, Lantz had a disagreement with her colonel after the truck rollover that killed the Marines and sailor. The Marines wrote the name of those killed on a barrier and put it at the entrance of the motor pool to memorialize the deceased. The colonel told them to take it down. Lantz talked to the colonel about keeping the barrier up; she thought it was good because it could help the Marines process their grief. He didn't budge. She spoke with the Marine Forces Pacific chaplain about it, and he advised her to write a point paper, a one-page argumentative paper. She wrote the paper and e-mailed it to the colonel. Later that afternoon, she went to see the colonel about something else. He still wouldn't change his mind, but he said it was the best point paper he had ever read.

After the Coast Guard Academy, Lantz went to work at the Naval Submarine Base New London, down the road in Groton, Connecticut, then to Okinawa, and then Norfolk, Virginia. She's traveled quite a distance since she joined in the Navy and has seen a lot. Iraq was the most challenging and rewarding time of her life. She's content now but not happy, she says. She has PTSD. Bob died at home of pancreatic cancer in 2011. Lantz was with him. At the time, Lantz was stationed at the sub base. She is grateful for the support she got during that period. The funeral was held at the First Presbyterian Church in Newport, Rhode Island, where Bob had served while Lantz was in seminary. Then they drove to the national cemetery in Cape Cod.

In 2011, the Legion of Valor—a group chartered by an act of Congress and composed of men who have been awarded the Medal of Honor, the Distinguished Service Cross, the Navy Cross, or the Air Force Cross—held an annual reunion at the submarine base in Groton. For this reunion, they asked for the use of the base chapel to remember their members who had died during the past year. Lantz was asked to speak at the memorial service. They had specifically requested that a combat chaplain speak.

Lantz reflected on death and dying with her comments: "As the wisdom of Solomon tells us, and as we sometimes somewhat glibly repeat, it wasn't his time to die. There is a time for everything, and a season for every activity under heaven. We have experienced the time for war, we have witnessed the time for death to come early to those whom we would rather have seen live a long and prosperous life.

"Some of you may have asked yourself the question, 'Why him and not me?' Your presence here today affirms that it wasn't your time. Instead you have been blessed with life and the time to remember. . . . My husband had a sticky note on his desk which read 'No one is gone until they are forgotten.' Today is a time to remember your colleagues, your friends, your band of brothers whose time to die came in the past year. The Psalmist says, 'The days of our life are seventy years, or perhaps eighty if we are strong.' It is time to grieve their passing and recognize they were blessed with strength in the fulfillment of their lives. We take the time to remember their valor, their service, their character, their quirks, their uniqueness."

Survivors Empowered Through Art

SPC Rachel McWilliams

In November 2004, SPC Rachel McWilliams, eighteen, was stationed at Fort Meade, Maryland, going through advanced training to become a broadcast journalist for the Army. It was Thanksgiving weekend, and she and her buddies had earned privileges to spend it off base.

Their plan was to watch movies and hang out. But McWilliams was tired from having duty all day in the barracks, so on the evening of November 27, she went to bed early in her hotel room.

The following morning, McWilliams woke up thinking she was having a nightmare, when in fact another soldier was sexually assaulting her. She wasn't conscious for most of it. It takes three alarm clocks to wake McWilliams in the morning, so it's no surprise she thought she was having a nightmare.

She tried to push the rapist off her and get away. He grabbed her hand, put it on his crotch, and said, "If you leave now, you'll never have this again."

McWilliams managed to escape outside. It was about 5 A.M. and bitter cold. She was dressed but wasn't wearing gloves and a hat to protect her from the freezing Maryland air. She wandered the streets for what seemed like hours, trying to wrap her head around what had just happened. What should she do? Who would believe her?

Her mom is from England and her American dad was an international sales representative. By the time she was thirteen, McWilliams had traveled to more than a dozen countries. She knew if she wanted to keep traveling and seeing the world, she would have to join the military. In addition, one of her grandfathers was a gunner for Britain in World War II, and she had been close to him. She had read a letter he wrote about his war experiences and wanted to travel and honor her grandfather. In 2003, at the age of seventeen, she got permission from her parents to enlist in the United States Army.

After the rape, McWilliams's excitement for the Army turned to apathy and numbness. This was not how she imagined her career as a soldier. In the months following the attack, McWilliams felt dirty and ashamed. "I'd wash myself in the maintenance sink because I couldn't bear the thought of showering with other soldiers, even if they were women," she said. "I just felt so dirty, like everyone could see the shame and disgust."

Nine times out of ten the victim knows her rapist. McWilliams's rapist was someone she knew and trusted—a friend. He was in her unit. When she went to the mall or chow with four or five other people, he was in the group. Now he had violated her.

The rape happened in November. McWilliams reported it in February. She had been too ashamed to come forward earlier, but it got to the point where she couldn't take seeing her rapist in formation and in the recreation room. "It just got to a breaking point for me," she said.

After finally gaining the courage to report the rape, she was greeted with accusations, victim-blaming, hate, badgering, and bullying. They acted as though she had encouraged and wanted the sexual behavior. What were you wearing? Had you been drinking? She spent hours over multiple days being interrogated by the Criminal Investigation Division with the "good cop/bad cop routine, more bad cop than good cop."

"I felt alone," she said. "I felt scared. I felt helpless. I just remember rocking back and forth in the chair when I was being interrogated. I'd cover my ears and repeat, 'No means no' over and over again."

Eventually, McWilliams was forced to drop the charges and was written up for fraternization. If she had other options, she didn't know what they were. No one told her. Instead, she was told there was no way the court would believe her. That she would have to go through multiple lie detector tests and then, when she was found to be lying (which they said they thought she was), she would go to jail and be dishonorably discharged.

The person who raped her had a different job than McWilliams, so when she was assigned to Korea as a broadcast journalist for the Armed Forces Network-Korea (AFN-K), she thought she was going to be safe. The people in her unit did a variety of jobs and were being assigned all over the place, including stateside and overseas. She had no idea that the rapist was going to Korea, too.

She was first assigned to a detachment for AFN-K in Daegu. Only five people were in the detachment, so she stayed in the barracks of another unit. McWilliams soon realized that again the chances of being raped were high. "I had to keep my door locked at all times," she said. "People would get so intoxicated they would go into someone else's room and fall asleep, steal things, or wreck the rooms. There were stories of women being sexually assaulted almost every week."

Even though she kept her door locked when in her room, she couldn't sleep for fear of assault. There was also the added stress of her supervisor, a noncommissioned officer, putting most of his work on her so he could slack off. He would have her do his assignments in addition to her own, so she would be up past midnight editing stories. She'd return to the barracks and not be able to sleep because of the assault. Then she would have to get up at 6 A.M. for physical training (PT). All this caused her to lose weight.

She lost so much weight that her roommate, who was in another unit, reported McWilliams's weight loss to her chaplain. The chaplain went up his chain of command, and soon the commander for her roommate's unit was calling AFN-K. "You rarely hear about a brigade commander contacting another unit's command to say they are not taking care of their own," McWilliams said. She was transferred up to AFN-K's headquarters at Yongsan Base in Seoul. The problem was, Yongsan was the headquarters of the U.S. military in South Korea and a big weekend destination for soldiers from other camps and bases to party and shop.

With medical treatment available and what appeared to be a safer environment, McWilliams thought she would finally start to recover. Although the Army had denied that she was assaulted, she now had access to therapy.

When a famous rock band went to Korea with the USO, McWilliams got along with the band so well that they arranged for her to go with them to all of their shows in Korea. While she was at a show at a different base, a soldier she knew from advanced individual training (AIT) told her that her rapist was stationed there. McWilliams met this soldier from AIT at the concert on a Wednesday night, called up her chain of command, and was told she was overreacting. They said there were more than 30,000 soldiers in Korea and that he was on a different base, so there was no way she'd ever see him again. Then she saw her rapist that Saturday at a bar in Itaewon, a shopping district right next to the base.

That night, McWilliams was with a group of friends who were medics from a different unit. She had confided in one of them that she had been assaulted. He was near the bathroom when she came out and locked eyes with her rapist. He saw her run back into the bathroom and the rapist take off, and knew instantly who he was. He tried to chase the rapist down but couldn't find him.

When she was finally coaxed out of the bathroom, McWilliams started drinking heavily. She drank one shot after another. Her friend managed to convince her to stop drinking, but she was already heavily intoxicated. On the way back to her barracks, she tripped on some steps and scratched her face. She was bleeding. She still has a scar on her cheek to remind her of that night. She remembers returning to her room and crying in bed.

Her coworker who lived in the room next door heard her and saw drops of blood. He called the military police because he thought someone had hurt McWilliams. He had just been promoted to sergeant, and in the end, her noncommissioned officer in charge (NCOIC), who was causing a lot of grief for her, had the coworker write her up for underage drinking as his first experience counseling someone.

Her direct supervisor, a female NCOIC, talked to McWilliams about her group counseling appointments in front of everyone after formation. She regularly told McWilliams that these appointments interfered with their mission and negatively impacted the unit's work. McWilliams was told to "get over it." The female NCOIC also publicly ridiculed McWilliams, calling her a pain in the ass, a flake, and a bad soldier.

She continued to run into her rapist at least once every two weeks. Yongsan, where she was stationed, was a huge base but McWilliams didn't feel safe anywhere. She would run into him in the most random places. She had thought she would be safe going to another country, that she wouldn't have to see him again. She felt as though she was being punished for something she did.

The Army was still unwilling to recognize the trauma stemming from the sexual assault. The Army psychiatrist said she had a personality disorder, not PTSD. She was immediately labeled as being bipolar and put on a mood stabilizer, antidepressant, and sleep medication. "I felt like a lab rat," she said. "They could never figure out a combination that wouldn't cause adverse side effects. I probably didn't need to be on that many medications, but I was so overwhelmed with anxiety, loss of sleep, numbness, that I just wanted it all to go away."

Her sergeant major was the only one who really supported McWilliams. He encouraged her to start group therapy and to increase the frequency of sessions. Yet it wasn't long before she started to have suicidal thoughts. "I wanted to end it," she recalled. "I was very close to it. I started cutting myself just so I could feel something."

Then came a turning point. McWilliams realized she needed to get out of the Army. To her, it was that or suicide. She went to her sergeant major, who was not her direct supervisor, for help. He had an open-door policy. Since she was in a small unit, she could just walk over to the sergeant major and ask him if he had time to talk, she said. It wasn't like a larger unit where she would have had to go up the chain of command. In the spring of 2006, she started the paperwork for an honorable discharge under Chapter 5-17, which some refer to as "at the convenience of the Army."

Her out-take session with her commander validated her decision to get out of the Army. She was told she was a failure and an embarrassment to the Army because she sought discharge. She was a quitter and would always be a quitter. She was an embarrassment to all women who had served.

Today, the effects of the sexual assault haunt her still. Because McWilliams—not the rapist—was written up for fraternization, she thought she was ineligible for benefits through the VA. She has PTSD as well as depression, seasonal affective disorder, and anxiety. She's hypervigilant. McWilliams is a single mom with a boy and a girl. Her son is the older of the two. For a time, when it was just her and her son, she'd sleep in the same bed with him to protect him. If a perpetrator got into the house or if there was a fire, she wondered how she would get the kids and herself out. She was strategizing for an emergency situation.

Because she doesn't really remember the rape, it's the events that occurred afterward—the blame and ridicule—that are the most traumatic. And winters are hard for her because she's reminded of that period of confusion when she wandered outside and was numb from the cold.

Once her career with the Army ended, McWilliams had a big decision to make. What next? She loved broadcast journalism, but the Army ruined that career for her. When she was in high school, her father had encouraged her to volunteer. That was something she was familiar with. Initially she went to Western Technical College in La Crosse, Wisconsin, to see how she would do taking college courses. She wasn't sure what she wanted to do, so she just took general education classes. She took a break from school to work, and then started at Winona State University in Winona, Minnesota. She also began working at various nonprofits, including work with at-risk youth, adults with mental illnesses, adults with developmental disabilities, and sexual assault (SA) and domestic violence (DV) victims. She soon realized SA/DV was her calling. In the midst of helping these victims, she began to heal.

"I think it hit home when I was working at a domestic abuse shelter in Oshkosh, Wisconsin, and met a girl who was severely beaten by her boyfriend," McWilliams said. "She was just a few years younger than I was at the time. She didn't have anyone, no family and no friends. It reminded me of when I reported. I didn't have anyone to hold my hand and tell me it was going to be okay or someone who could connect me to resources. It was then that I realized that I needed to work with victims and help them on their journey to recovery."

In college, McWilliams took all online classes because she couldn't handle on-campus classes. Also, she's older than most students and has different priorities. And there were too many students, making her unable to focus. She was hypervigilant, constantly aware of her surroundings. She compared it to sitting in a restaurant and being aware of what everyone around you is doing—what each person is drinking, eating, etc. There are waitresses, waiters, busboys, hostesses. She would hear every sound. Now imagine being on a college campus and trying to be aware of everything going on around you. Online classes gave her the chance to take courses on her own terms—in her house, in her pajamas, an hour at a time.

Whenever she has an anxiety attack, it's like there's a tiny hole in her head and the whole world is trying to fit into that hole. Her mind races and it's hard for her to focus, pay attention, and interact. One time she had to leave a birthday party her son was attending because there was too much commotion. She has since gotten a service dog, which has helped immensely with her fight or flight response.

During her undergraduate program, she had health issues and ended up diagnosed with epilepsy. It was then that McWilliams realized the importance of college services like disability and student support. Before she was diagnosed with epilepsy, she had no idea that disability services helped students with all sorts of medical conditions. She thought it was just for people with learning or physical disabilities. She didn't realize they helped students with mental illnesses and other conditions that affect schoolwork.

McWilliams was able to get a private room and extended test times, which helped with both the anxiety aspect of her PTSD and her seizures. In a private room, she could read the questions and answers aloud without distracting or being distracted by others. That was also when she realized she wanted to work in student affairs—whether in veterans services, disability services, or some other type of student support services. She was accepted into the Student Affairs Administration in Higher Education program at the University of Wisconsin–La Crosse and got a temporary graduate assistantship position in the Violence Prevention Office working at both UW and Western Technical College.

McWilliams also got a graduate assistant position as a violence prevention specialist at two other colleges. It's the only job she has been able to hold down since the rape. Educating faculty, staff, and students helps her because she knows what she does is making a difference.

"Hey, I threw a grenade, shot a .50-cal., trained in hand-to-hand combat, and I was still raped," she tells her audience. "It can happen to anyone." Although she's moved on from that position, she still is asked to do classroom presentations and to work with the colleges on different events relating to sexual assault.

Viewing the documentary *The Invisible War* aided her healing. The film has rape victims telling their stories. McWilliams helped organize a panel for the viewing. The movie lit a fire under her. For eight years she had pushed her trauma to the side. Although it was still too hard to deal with, she finally understood that she wasn't alone: "I realized I'm not one of few, I'm one of many."

Before seeing *The Invisible War,* she didn't really speak out. She suffered in silence, suffocating with PTSD. When she did speak in the schools, she would tell survivors that she was assaulted, but she said it in such a way that it came across as a superficial comment. She never went into great depth with anyone, not even her therapist. It was the documentary that caused her to advocate outside schools, speaking to organizations and hosting community events. McWillliams had spoken about rape, but she didn't realize it was an actual problem until she saw the documentary. "The way they treated me, it was like I was the only one that it ever happened to," she said. "The documentary showed me that it was actually an epidemic and that thousands go through the exact same thing or something similar every year."

After seeing the documentary, a weight was lifted off her shoulders. It was validating to hear other stories of women going through what she had been experiencing. She had no support when she reported her rape. "If I make one victim realize that she's not alone, I've done my job," she said.

She started looking for different nonprofits. She connected with the Wisconsin Coalition Against Sexual Assault (WCASA), where she is on their Survivors and Allies Task Force. She has also conducted training for numerous regions within WCASA and has held workshops during conferences and gatherings.

She felt she had a new calling. If other brave women could talk about their trauma, so could she. She wanted to get to that place. Since watching *The Invisible War,* McWilliams has spoken about her rape on numerous occasions and finds it rewarding when people come up to her after she presents to say that what she is doing is making a difference, whether it's making an ally or making a victim feel they are not alone. Or having people say they had no idea there was such a problem in the military.

Perhaps McWilliams's greatest venture to date has been the establishment of her nonprofit, Survivors Empowered Through

Art (SETA). McWilliams received a scholarship to attend a military sexual trauma summit in Washington, D.C., in April 2013. There she met other MST survivors for the first time. She was so inspired by their stories that she began to collect the stories and poetry of survivors and their loved ones to turn into a theater project called *Speaking Out: Why I Stand.*

As word about the project spread, McWilliams and her peers decided to make the theater project a nonprofit. Brian Lewis, one of the male survivors featured in *The Invisible War*, came up with the name, "Survivors Empowered Through Art." Through this project, sexual assault advocates, community members, and survivors portray and read aloud their stories and poems on stage before an audience.

McWilliams now has three main projects. The first is the theater project. Another is Project Retrospect: Flipping the Script on Rape, a photography project. The third is Stepping Stones: Our Path to Healing, a glass bricks–painting workshop for survivors.

McWilliams was finding her niche. Growing up in different countries, she had been able to visit a lot of museums and see many plays, and she understood the effectiveness of a play to get across a message. *SETA Speaking Out: Why I Stand* was a play for survivors to express themselves. Survivors shared their stories and poems with McWilliams. Then she picked which ones would be performed. McWilliams came up with the set design. Community members auditioned to portray the survivors and loved ones on stage. These stories came from all over the world.

As a child, McWilliams had loved the arts. In high school, if anyone needed to find her, she was probably in the art room, either sculpting or painting. So it seemed natural for her to expand from theater into visual art.

In Project Retrospect, people from across the country e-mail questions to her. If they are a survivor, it might be a question they have wanted to ask their rapist. If they are a community member or ally, it may be a question that popped into their head while watching the news or reading an article. They submit the question, and McWilliams goes into the community and takes photographs of the questions spelled out in Scrabble tiles, bottle caps, on chalkboards, and so forth.

Her newest project, Stepping Stones: Our Path to Healing, uses glass blocks. Individuals will paint pictures and/or write something positive on the glass, something that helped them go from victim to survivor or from survivor to warrior. McWilliams plans to string lights through the blocks inside a gallery, making a path and lighting it up.

She also came up with the idea of a "rejuvenation room" at WCASA's conferences. If someone gets triggered, they can go to the room to relax. The rejuvenation room might have yoga or music going on, or glass blocks to paint. This was part of the conferences and gatherings with WCASA.

While working on her art projects, McWilliams has continued learning how to heal, which has meant adjusting at times. "Everybody has to take baby steps when healing," McWilliams said. "People need to find out what their baby steps are." McWilliams went from not talking about her rape to talking about it all the time. "If you're a survivor, you don't have to feel bad about speaking out or not speaking out to a friend or therapist."

One great thing about SETA is that in all of the projects, survivors can take part while remaining anonymous. There are assumptions that healing means speaking out and putting your face in front of an issue, or that these things are required to make a difference. "I enjoy getting e-mails from survivors who have taken part in the projects, even when it is something as simple as e-mailing a question for the photography project," McWilliams said. "Then they see the photos of them on Facebook or up in galleries. They know that is their question or their glass block and [that] they are helping to raise awareness."

McWilliams knows healing is a lifelong process. She will have PTSD her entire life. But she also knows she has put herself in a better place and she can see that light.

"Healing means knowing my PTSD and my triggers and trying to acknowledge them," McWilliams said. "To be able to face them instead of not talking about them. Having a positive way of getting through an anxiety attack."

The "F" Word

SPC Alicia Philson

"We will be restless until we rest in God."
—St. Augustine

As a combat medic, Army SPC Alicia Philson saw her share of gruesome things. She witnessed Iraqi nationals caught in the crosshairs. One guy had his guts hanging out and another was throwing up blood. She watched as little kids covered in shrapnel ran toward her in tears.

Philson isn't the squeamish type, so a lot of what she saw didn't damage her emotionally as it did some soldiers. In fact, those attacks had little to do with the PTSD she experienced when she returned home. She attributes her PTSD instead to watching her fellow soldiers—other Americans—getting maimed and killed. The difference is that Philson had no relationship with the Iraqis. When they came to her for help, they were nameless. They were patients with body parts who needed medical attention. On the other hand, the wounds and deaths of American GIs got to her, especially when they were people she knew.

Philson was in the 630th MP Company, living and working with the 126th Infantry in and around various neighborhoods of Baghdad. They were each other's quick reaction force, which meant that anytime there was an attack on the 126th, her company responded, and vice versa.

June 21, 2007, started out like any other day. Before her mission, Philson gathered with her squad, said the Lord's Prayer, and kissed the photo of her daughter, Tiani, that she carried with her.

"The whole day was insane," she recalled. Philson, twenty-three, and other soldiers in the 630th MP Company were on patrol with Iraqi police in Ademiyah, a neighborhood of Baghdad, when they got a call that the 126th was under attack. A Bradley truck had been blown up and six soldiers were dead. Philson's unit needed to cordon off a four-way intersection down the street from the 126th. Each of the four vehicles in Philson's unit blocked a road to keep people from coming and going. They continuously moved their trucks so they weren't sitting targets. Nevertheless, a rocket-propelled grenade hit one of the trucks.

"What the fuck was that?" yelled the squad leader.

The driver of Philson's vehicle moved their truck to recover the hit vehicle and its occupants. They parked on the passenger side, facing the opposite direction. When Philson opened her door, they were still taking fire. She thought, *Fuck, I have to go get them. I'm going to die.*

Philson's roommate was in the truck that had been hit. Someone shouted that she had been decapitated. Philson instinctively put on her blue latex gloves and ran to the damaged Humvee. The window on the passenger's side had been shattered. Philson watched as the truck commander, Sgt. Doug Quick, opened his door and stumbled out. His face and the front of his uniform were covered with soot and blood. His eyes were full of fright.

In wartime, Philson saw things that she could recognize as either right or wrong. Seeing Quick covered in black, with the white of his eyes popping out—this was wrong. *We're at fucking war now*, she thought.

Quick got up and pointed his weapon in the wrong direction. The explosion had shaken him up and he was disoriented. Philson ran to him and threw him down on the ground. "Hey, you all right?" Philson asked.

"Yeah, I'm good," he said. "Go get them. Go get them."

Philson had a wad of gauze. She wiped the soot off Quick's face. He was peppered with shrapnel but had no major bleeding. She knew he would be okay to transfer back to safety. She led him the ten or so feet from his truck to hers and shut the door behind him. She felt a bullet whiz past her helmet.

As she maneuvered around the kill zone, her gunner, SPC Joel Trimmer, was shooting at her six while SPC John Deweese, another gunner, had her twelve and was lighting shit up in the direction the rounds were coming from.

She went back to her roommate's truck, to the passenger's side, and peeked in. The RPG had gone through her fellow soldier, then hit the radio mount and engine. Her roommate's petite body (100 pounds soaking wet) had been knocked over. All that was left of her head was her ponytail. The women always wear their hair in a bun, but when her roommate was hit, her hair came down. There was nothing else left to see. Philson didn't think too much about the hair at the time because she was so busy, but she remembered it later. She just knew it was wrong that the hair was down.

Philson wanted to grab her roommate but there was nothing she could do for her, which was difficult. As a medic, she was trained to bring everyone back whole, and when she hadn't done that, regardless of whether she could save someone or not, she felt like she had failed. It would take Philson a long time to get over those feelings, to shed the guilt—if ever.

Philson had a choice to either pull the corpse out of the truck or help the soldiers who were still alive. It didn't matter that her roommate was her friend. How she felt about the situation didn't count in war. Philson shouted aloud to herself, "Stop! You can't do anything!"

She crouched behind the Humvee because they were still taking fire. Medics usually get an M9 and a shotgun. Philson put her M9 on black, meaning the safety was off, so it was ready to go, and then rolled her eyes at her relative lack of firepower. She jumped back into her truck and quickly assessed Quick, who had taken shrapnel all over. She continued his treatment, making sure his extremities were all working. They drove to a combat outpost, still treating Deweese and Quick, where an Apache was waiting to transfer the wounded.

Philson didn't know the big picture at the time. The squad leader was talking to their commander, who was about thirty seconds out. The commander told them to leave her roommate because they would be coming for the damaged truck and towing it back. The commander arrived before they left the scene, and the truck was towed to an Apache.

When she got back to base (the old ministry of defense, or MoD), Philson and one of her roommate's best friends were talking. The friend wanted to know what happened. Before Philson could finish, the friend said, "I'm so fucking pissed you left her."

Philson was lonely for the rest of her tour in Iraq. She felt like she couldn't talk to anyone about what happened. She talked to her husband at the time, but it was hard to express what happened to someone who wasn't there. And it was too hard to talk to those who were there because they didn't want to relive it.

"We were surrounded by war," she said. "Every day I thought I was going to die. Even if you're not in that situation, it's horrible if you don't have people around you who are supportive. Your command is important, especially when people are trying to kill you."

Philson said her command was "freaking awesome." Her commander, Capt. Eric Tangeman (now a major), pulled her aside after the attack to chat with her and to see how she was doing. She tried to bullshit him with meaningless conversation, but he called her on it. "No, how are you *really* doing?" he asked.

Philson and others in her platoon went to group counseling, and they had access to a bereavement counselor and a chaplain. Tangeman pointed out people he thought were affected by the attack. "He knew us," Philson said. "It made all the difference to me. Someone actually fucking got me and actually gave a shit. I'm not just a soldier to him. I'm an actual person."

Years later she would have anxiety attacks in the middle of the night and call Tangeman. He was still there for her. She would say, "I'm fucking freaking out, sir," and he would talk her through it. "He had no obligation to do that, but he's just a genuine person and an incredible major," she said. "I feel blessed to have served for him. . . . If you feel like they are taking care of you, it makes it easier. Mostly you want to know that you're loved and appreciated. Who fucking knows why we're there?"

Knowing that she was there for a reason and willing to die for something was important to Philson. As a mom, she needed to know her sacrifice meant something. But at the same time, she couldn't think about her daughter, Tiani. She had to keep her emotions at bay. She'd tell herself she was there for the soldier next to her. If she had emotions for Tiani, she wouldn't be able to do the mission. Instead, she would constantly miss her or be happy that she had a daughter, in which case the floodgates would open and tears would flow. She would start feeling things—and she couldn't feel things like that in war. It was much easier to numb herself and continue the mission.

Immediately following the attack on June 21, Philson dug in and kept her nose to the ground. She was fine the day of the firefight. Her body was running on adrenaline.

"You all right, Doc?" other soldiers would ask.

"Yeah, I'm all right," she answered.

They sat around, smoked, and traded war stories.

The evening of the attack, Philson had night terrors. She woke up shaking and convulsing. She ran to another soldier's room and started crying. A group of them went to the smoke pit. They smoked while she cried. There she was, in the middle of the night, hanging out with infantry guys. She hadn't brushed her teeth. She didn't have on a bra. And she was crying.

"We'll get them for you, Philson," the guys said. "Don't you worry, little girl." (Philson is five feet one.) They were trying to protect her the only way they knew how. Talk of revenge made her feel better at the time.

Some of the infantrymen wouldn't look her way. She thought she could read their minds. "Fucking female. Always crying." Yet she only cried twice in war, that night and at the memorial service.

Philson quickly learned it didn't do any good to dwell on dead comrades. There would be time for that later, when she got home. Right now she had a war to fight, and it wasn't going to stop because she was having a shitty day. Philson likes to remind people, "Everyone deploys; only some go to the war."

When she returned to Bamberg, Germany, home of the 630th MP Company, Philson had thirty days of leave. She stayed drunk the entire time. The June 21 attack took place fourteen months into Philson's deployment. Her unit was supposed to have boots back on the ground in the States on June 8, but they got extended. Philson arrived home in August.

She left Tiani when she was five months old and returned when she was a year and a half. When she got home, she didn't know how to be a mom to her daughter. "I saw so much shit," she said. "I remember thinking, how the fuck am I going to hold her? She's happy and innocent. My hands have been bloodied with war. I didn't know how to bond with her. She was so small. She couldn't talk. She would look at me like she wanted me to hold her. I looked at her like I had nothing to give her." Philson felt like she couldn't be a mother, yet she was.

Not being able to nurture her child because she was so "fucked up in the head" was one of the reasons Philson drank for so long. "I couldn't cope with not being able to cope," she said.

Aiding in her binge drinking was her then husband, a heavy drinker himself. Philson wasn't a drinker before the war, but when she came back and wanted a drink, her husband was on board. "Fuck yeah," he'd say. "Let's get this party started." They'd go through more than a gallon of Jack Daniels in a weekend.

During those thirty days of leave, Philson drank from the moment she got up until she went to bed. She didn't know how to love her daughter, so she bought her things. She hung out with the other soldiers from her unit who had seen the same horrors she saw. She felt closer to them than she did to her husband and daughter. "I know for a fact that at the time they felt closer to me than their wives. I wasn't the cheating type. I was married and had a baby. They looked at me like I was their brother."

After a year and a half in Germany, Philson was reassigned to Tripler Army Medical Center in Hawaii, where she got a divorce and was medically discharged from the Army for uterine adhesions and PTSD. It wasn't until she went through the medical board process for discharge that she started talking about some of her horrific experiences as a combat medic.

The night before her medical board interview, Philson had to work a twenty-four-hour shift. By the time her interview rolled around, she was "crazy emotional" from not sleeping. As soon as the interviewer started asking her questions, she broke down. She was sent to psych for an evaluation. She had a panic attack and called the commanding officer she had deployed with. He talked her through her panic attack and encouraged her to talk to the psychiatrist. The medical board determined that Philson had PTSD and was an alcoholic.

At this time, Philson was drinking three bottles of wine a night. Drinking was the only way she could sleep. She'd wake up at 4:00 in the morning, get her two daughters ready for day care (she'd had her second daughter, Carly, following her deployment to Iraq), sit in traffic, drop them off, go to the clinic where she worked, stay for eight to twelve hours, pick up her kids at 5:30 or 6:00, sit in traffic again, make them dinner, bathe them, read them a story, and then drink. "That was me just surviving," she said. "I didn't know how to be happy. I didn't know it was okay for me to be happy." She'd wake up at 4:00 the next morning and do it all over again. That was Philson bottoming out.

"I looked so good on the outside," she said. She was an NCO (sergeant) in the Army and a single mom. Her kids looked great, she worked out, her house was immaculate, and she was in a position of power. "But on the inside, I was a fucking mess," she said. She started counseling with the person who evaluated her as having PTSD. After she was discharged from the Army, it would take six months for the VA to get back to her with a referral for a new counselor.

Philson had no plan for transitioning from the military to civilian life, or for healing postwar. So she drank and partied. The Army sent her to a substance abuse program. She attended the program for a few weeks but stopped going because she was happy drinking. The kids were dressed, the house was clean. She was doing what she had to do. Philson continued drinking for six to seven months after she got out of the Army. She went on unemployment, got retirement, partied, and threw it all away. She had lost the only identity that she really knew—being a soldier.

"I put being a soldier before everything . . . family, marriage, liver," she said. "I put everything into being a soldier, and they told me I couldn't be one anymore."

Her next job would be to heal, but how? "I didn't know how to heal," Philson said.

She was about to get some help from an unlikely person. One of the female soldiers stationed at Tripler started sending Philson text messages about how much God loved her and that Jesus was her savior. "I was so irritated," she said. "I get it. Get off my shit."

She knew she was unhappy and didn't know how to fix it. The drinking wasn't working. Something had to change. She no longer had the excuse of a crummy husband or the Army. Philson was the only reason—she was her only excuse.

It's easy for soldiers to have PTSD and not deal with it. You have to keep going. The mission always comes first. But Philson didn't have those military missions anymore. All she had left were herself, her daughters, and a bottle of Jack. Her daughters weren't the reason this happened. They were "super-awesome kids." She couldn't blame them. She was running out of excuses. "I knew I needed to fix my shit. I was used to having all these excuses," Philson said. "God fixed that for me. He took out all the reasons I hid behind."

She had a little bit of faith while at war. She said the Lord's Prayer every day before she went outside the wire, but she wasn't aware that God would forgive her and that if He forgave her, then she certainly could forgive herself. "I saw faith as a crutch," she said. "I need Him right now, so I'm going to lean on Him." When she left Iraq, she preferred to lean on Jack Daniels—for a while.

But Philson was lonely, and the soldier kept texting her. Soon Philson started to pay attention. She began to go to church and to hear that God loves her. He really did. And the love was unconditional. She didn't know how to accept God's love, but figured if he could love her that much, it was okay for her to love herself, too. "I was finally okay with me being happy, allowing me to be happy," she said.

Like most things in life, however, faith is not a constant. It ebbs and flows. She would have a happy moment when her faith would be strong, followed by a memory of her roommate's death and a period of shattered faith. Because what God would allow such mutilation and violence? Still she persevered in her faith. Then one day she said she just felt the Lord inside her. She knows she's broken, imperfect, and is okay with that.

"I was so angry at myself for everything that I went through," Philson said. "I was so angry at life. When it came right down to it, I wasn't ready to forgive myself for not saving my roommate or for leaving my five-month-old daughter and going off to war. I just hated who I was. I didn't know how to make it better. That's when I started getting closer to God." Partying wasn't working. Her marriage hadn't worked. Having her kids around her all the time wasn't working.

"I knew I wanted more," she said. "I wanted to be happy." Philson realized that God had forgiven her for her sins. That's why Jesus died on the cross. It was through this revelation that she realized He loved her so much and so unconditionally that she could forgive herself. It took a while. She went to church for a year without talking to anyone, without getting involved. But once she forgave herself and let Him into her heart, her life totally changed.

Life's not all roses. Her circumstances didn't change. She still was divorced. Her kids still drove her crazy. Some days her sister, Kuuipo (Ipo for short), hated her. The VA had still "fucked me over." But she was okay with having PTSD and her kids being wild because she had peace. Even when it seemed like there was nothing she could do about a situation, there was something. She could pray and ask for patience.

"For me, it wasn't until I lost everything that I held dear—marriage, Army, identity, family—when that happened I was like, fuck, now what? Instead of being bitter about it, I thought there are so many things for me to still be grateful for and that I don't need material things for me to be happy. I have Jesus, and whatever happens He will bring me through it. I dig Jesus."

Philson is grateful for all of the horrible things that have happened in her life because she realizes they made her the person she is now. She's happy with who she is. "I don't always like my circumstances, but I'm so blessed by the opportunities the Lord has given me in life," she said. "Not everyone can appreciate a warm shower. I sure fucking can."

She anticipates struggling with alcoholism for the rest of her life because it's easy for her to relapse. She got drunk on the anniversary of her roommate's death but still feels she's in a better place because she has faith. She has family and friends who get her and get that she's not perfect. She may have an anxiety attack and drink. It doesn't change who she is. It doesn't make her a bad person.

The memory of her roommate keeps Philson moving forward, but it didn't at first. People get stuck. "I felt like I needed to be sad and I needed to hang onto this [memory]," she said. Her roommate didn't get to finish her life. "Why the fuck should I be happy?" Philson asked. "It's not fair that I should be happy." Happiness was always tinged with guilt.

Now Philson knows it's okay. Her roommate would want her to be happy. Philson has come to the conclusion that it's okay to honor her roommate and to have a drink on the anniversary of her death. It's all right to be sad for her roommate and for what Philson continues to go through as a survivor. "I know she died," Philson said. "The shit was fucked up for me, too. It's ok to feel that way. The people that I deployed with are my family."

What seems to have changed is that Philson now tries to honor her roommate's memory by taking care of herself instead of being destructive with her own life. She realizes that she wasn't happy because of what she was and wasn't doing in life. She was still drinking but going to church to hear the Word and to get her Jesus fix; then she would party some more. But she also started reading her Bible more, journaling, and jotting down scripture. She knew she wanted things to change but it took a while. It didn't happen overnight.

Helping her get more involved in church were her daughters, who wanted to hang out with the kids in the children's Sunday school. That got Philson talking with the moms. But she was afraid of being around Christians. Still in a military community, she thought the women were all perfect military spouses, whereas she was this broken alcoholic running on the fumes of her Army career. Much to her surprise, they accepted her. Some of them also had broken lives and were able to overcome issues because they let the Lord carry them. The other wives knew they'd be OK because they trusted in God. "I wanted that faith," Philson said.

She started going to Bible study and working out with the wives. She had been drinking, getting fat, feeling gross. Now she was starting to feel and look better. She was doing all these things to feel good. She was working on her inner and outer self. She made friends with women who weren't alcoholics, and she lost the need to drink and get wasted. Whenever Philson has a problem now, her friends guide her in a healthy direction, in a direction that she wants to go.

"Blessed are those who mourn, for they will be comforted," she said, quoting Matthew 5:4. "The thing about the Bible is that it's not a book about how everything will be fine. It tells you that you will go through hard times but that He'll help you through it. The Bible has an answer for a healthy way to live."

Scriptures like James 4:8, "Come near to God and he will come near to you," spoke to her. "Because I didn't know any better, I thought God had abandoned me, but he was there the whole time," she said. "He was just waiting for me to come to Him. Once I decided I wanted to be close to Him, he was there. . . . I'm still broken and no supermodel, but inside I felt the difference," she said. "He welcomed me. I just felt a joy inside."

Philson's sister, Ipo, has been instrumental in helping her. They'd hang out after work and watch television. Philson remembers watching a show where the characters were breaking down doors and questioning a suspect. She said to whomever was sitting in the room, "Oh yeah, I remember we were interrogating someone and he wouldn't talk, so we put a 9mm to his head." Her family would respond, "That's crazy." Then she'd get quiet and not talk for hours. She'd just shut down. She described some of her experience as a "poison stuck in me, and sometimes it would ooze out."

In 2013, Philson hit bottom again. Like a lot of veterans, her road to recovery has been a roller coaster. She was evicted from the home she was renting because the landlord wanted it back. She wasn't getting paid by the VA. Her car was repossessed, and she didn't have a job. She was overweight and not dealing with her PTSD.

Yet the joy never left her. She was still incredibly grateful for everything. She and her daughters moved in with her sister, and Philson and her sister forged a better relationship.

She got out of the Army in 2011. In 2013, she still didn't know her VA rating. She called her member of Congress, but that didn't help. But she wasn't letting that take her joy. She had to lose everything to realize all she needed was God. "Now that I have Him, it doesn't matter what I lose or have," she said. "He sustains me."

Philson has since gotten a rating of 70 percent. She's remarried and living in the Sacramento area with her husband and three children. She hopes to go to college someday to study nursing.

What Doesn't Kill You Makes You Stronger

Tech Sgt. Jennifer Norris

THE FIRST TIME JENNIFER NORRIS WAS SEXUALLY ASSAULTED, SHE had no rank. She was twenty-four and had just signed up with the Air National Guard in South Portland, Maine. The recruiter was having a party for the new recruits. Because this recruiter had a great reputation, Norris had no reservations about going to his house. She was excited to meet everyone.

However, when she got to the party she was the only recruit present. *Maybe they haven't arrived yet*, she thought. As it turns out, "they" never planned to go to the party. The only people there that night were a couple who lived next door, Norris, and the recruiter.

The recruiter wanted to play drinking games, like Quarters, and pressured Norris to participate. She got angry and wanted to leave. She had a half-hour drive home. But when she stood up to leave, she felt dizzy, so she lay down on the couch in the recruiter's living room and passed out. She woke up when he picked up her limp body and carried her to his bedroom. He raped her and then rolled her over.

When she woke the following morning and was able to move, she grabbed her clothes and ran out. She went home and showered and cried. What just happened? Later she realized she had been drugged.

That so-called "party" was in 1996, two weeks after Norris had signed up for the Air Force. "I hadn't even gone to basic training," she said. Also, she was celibate and not on birth control. She went to the doctor, not to report the rape but to find out if she had gotten any diseases. She found out she did have medical issues related to the rape.

She didn't report the rape because she didn't want it to affect her military career. "What was I supposed to say? I was raped by your recruiter."

She started drinking heavily but managed to soldier on and do what she had to do to get by. In the meantime, she avoided the recruiter and his building at all cost. Later in the year, before basic training, Norris stopped drinking and smoking. She was gung-ho about joining the Air Force and kicking butt. She loved the esprit de corps, getting involved in something much bigger than herself, and marching in uniform. "I was like GI Jen," she said. At boot camp, her drill instructors recognized that she was a leader, so they made her a follower. It was a tough transitional time. She was twenty-four compared to the rest of the recruits who were eighteen. She also had a bachelor's degree and had worked as a social worker.

Following basic training, Norris went to satellite and wideband communications school at Keesler Air Force Base in Biloxi, Mississippi, to learn how to install and configure equipment. There were 10 female to 200 male students. It was like a "meat market," Norris said. "The male airmen came onto the women all the time."

The school program was six months. In her classes, where she was often the only female, she was belittled and treated poorly. "The more excited I was, the worse I was treated," she said. One female airman reported her instructor for making derogatory comments to her. Norris said the school went on a witch hunt to get her out and succeeded. "There was no way in hell I was going to report anything," she said.

Her career field was more like the Army than the Air Force because it was combat communications. That means she was in with a tougher crowd than usual. She was two weeks from graduation when it was her turn to be assaulted. She went into the satellite communications van to take a test. Her instructor came in behind her, shut the door, and she started a maintenance loop. Then he smashed Norris into the equipment. He leaned up against her and said, "Let me help you."

"Leave me alone," Norris said, pushing him away. "What the fuck? What the fuck?" She took him off guard. He was surprised that she resisted.

She finished her maintenance test but was anxious and her hands were shaking. She couldn't leave the van until he gave her permission. Then she went back to class. He told her to stay afterward. That's when she learned she had failed the class because of her poor attitude.

"Why are you doing this to me?" she asked through her tears.

"I'll reconsider if you show up tomorrow morning an hour before everyone else," he said.

That wasn't going to happen. She went to the Air National Guard liaison instead of class. Norris didn't want to report the instructor for assaulting her because that would mean the end of her career. She only had two weeks until graduation. So she told the liaison that she wasn't feeling well; she was homesick and depressed. She didn't see her predator again and went on to graduate.

While she was in tech school, Norris met another Maine guardsman whose cousin was sexually assaulted by a recruiter. It turned out it was the same recruiter who had raped her. Norris called the recruiter and told him that when she returned to Maine, she was going to press charges against him. The recruiter quit his job of eighteen years and moved to North Carolina. She returned to Maine thinking she would be safe.

Norris excelled when she got back to the 265th Combat Communications Squadron in Maine. She earned the Superior Performer and Airman of the Year awards. But those accolades were short-lived after she was assaulted yet again.

In 1998, Norris had started working full-time for a master sergeant who was superintendent of the maintenance squadron. He began showing favoritism toward her and giving her leadership positions. He was setting her up so he could attack her every chance he got. This lasted for a year. He would have her work by herself in the warehouse or run errands with him. He'd make his move and she'd push him off; he'd come back and say, "I don't want you anyway, bitch. Your tits are too small."

This kind of treatment occurred on a daily basis. Norris didn't want to report him because he was the commanding officer's right-hand man. If she said something, she would most likely get kicked out of the Air Force. But the assaults escalated and the master sergeant, who was married and had three kids, started to stalk her.

Norris likened what was going on to a "domestic violence relationship that I couldn't leave." She went on an operational readiness exercise (ORE) to Brunswick, Maine. The master sergeant was there, too. When the airmen weren't working, they were having squadron parties. Drinking was a big part of the culture. She went to one keg party with friends and found herself unknowingly standing outside the master sergeant's barracks room. He dragged her into his room, pulled her onto his bed, and assaulted her. He was drunk and hadn't shut the door all the way. A friend heard Norris's scream for help and saved her from rape.

Before this attack, Norris had been managing to avoid the master sergeant. They worked opposite shifts, which made it easier to steer clear of him. But a couple days before the party, he gave her a three-page handwritten letter in which he urged her to give in to his sexual desires. In the note he wrote that he would see her at the (mandatory) Thursday-night squadron party.

After the attempted rape, Norris was devastated. She was depressed and beaten down. No one reported anything even though they saw what happened. When she returned from ORE, she received the Superior Airman award, but she overslept that morning and wasn't there to receive it because she dreaded seeing the master sergeant. Sometime later, the Airman of the Year award was given to another airman.

One day in August 1998, another NCO whom Norris had been working with asked her why she didn't give a shit about serving in the military anymore. She had gone from super troop, someone who was totally dedicated to military life, to smoking and not working out. She had gone from having a purpose in life and constantly improving herself to experiencing intense anxiety and questioning her career choice. Simply by asking this, the NCO opened the floodgates and she told him everything that had happened. Norris begged him not to tell the commanding officer because she was certain her career would be over. He said that if she didn't report it, he would. So she reported the assaults to the commanding officer.

At first he said the accusations were alleged. Then she gave him the note the master sergeant had written to her. The commanding officer stood up and, with anger in his voice, said, "He betrayed me." About the same time, the commanding officer learned about the recruiter and the reason behind his leaving the Air Force. He believed Norris. "When you don't say anything, that means you're not going to say anything and it escalates," she realized. Now she had spoken up.

From her relatively short time in the Air Force, she reported four predators. Her superiors didn't have jurisdiction over the recruiter because he had moved to another state. Nor did they have jurisdiction over the active-duty airman in Mississippi. She could only report and follow through with a tech sergeant who was sexually harassing her on National Guard weekends and with the master sergeant. She proceeded with what she thought was justice, the right thing, going up the chain of command. Turns out that was a joke.

After her claims of sexual harassment against the master sergeant were made public, other female airmen told her they were assaulted, too. Norris couldn't believe it. "I just went through hell because you didn't say anything," she said. "You better get your fucking asses into the CO's office and tell him what happened to you." The commanding officer filed an EEO complaint against the master sergeant. It got knocked down from attempted rape to sexual harassment. The master sergeant would have an administrative hearing.

The commanding officer had Norris type up everything that had happened. While she was writing her report, the master sergeant came looking for her and wanted to know what she was doing. Norris went into fight-or-flight mode. She jumped up and went to her commander's office. She told the commander she couldn't stay there anymore and asked to be transferred. She was sent to headquarters in Augusta, Maine. After she finished her federal job, she went back to work in the civilian world. Around this time she started to drink more and to fall apart.

After a six-month period, the administrative hearing was held in March 1999. Both men, master sergeant and tech sergeant, settled and copped a plea so the results wouldn't become a matter of public record. The master sergeant got fired and lost one stripe. He was also transferred and forced out at twenty years.

Norris didn't have evidence against the tech sergeant, only her own testimony and that of other victims, so he just got kicked out of the Maine Guard and received a letter of reprimand. He joined the New Hampshire National Guard and later went to work for the Pentagon. She knows this because she saw him at a conference where he was in charge of all the combat communications units. So both the men whom she reported retired with full benefits and never went on the sex offender registry.

Norris returned to her squadron in South Portland and described it as a "snake pit" where she was instantly ostracized as well as punished. The Airman of the Year award she had earned was taken away from her in retaliation and someone else's name was put on the plaque. Norris also was pulled from her leadership positions. People she had been training were now training her. Eventually she was made to work on the same equipment day in and day out and was isolated. In an effort to further humiliate her, guys would hug the wall when they walked by her.

"I know it sounds like a nightmare, and it was," she said. "Imagine this happening to an eighteen-year-old. It's like bullying. And in the military you can't quit. You can't call in sick. There are no laws. It's insidious. They can do outright things or underhanded things. That's dangerous. I'd been raped, and they all turned on me for being the bad guy," she said. "The betrayal is what beats your soul down. I had to transfer to escape what was like a domestic violence relationship that I couldn't get a divorce from."

In 2000, when she told her unit her dad was dying of cancer, they said that could take forever. She didn't want to go in on guard weekends because that's when she got the most harassment. She asked to make up the guard weekends during the week. Others did; it was no big deal. They wanted to force her to take a leave of absence that would have impacted her active-duty time. The commanding officer eventually let her take some weekends off to spend with her dad, and she made up those days during the week. To do so, she had to take vacation days from her civilian job. She was turned in to her commander for arriving at 7:00 instead of 6:00 or 6:30.

In 2001, Norris got transferred to Otis Air National Guard Base, Buzzards Bay, Massachusetts, for four years. It was a full-time job. She was so willing to escape the abusive squadron up north that she would drive four hours from Maine to Massachusetts, to the closest communications squadron. She thought the new location would represent a new start, but her reputation as a troublemaker preceded her. She talked to the commander in Massachusetts about filling a slot—she wanted to work at the satellite communications center. She was told she had it. But because she had a reputation for causing problems, she was treated poorly and belittled. They gave her the most menial jobs.

When she arrived at Otis, she was informed she would have to go back to Keesler for more training. Keesler was where she had been attacked by the tech sergeant but couldn't do anything about it because he was outside her jurisdiction.

But now, as soon as she saw her perpetrator at the NCO club, a blind fury kicked in. She needed closure. The same night she confronted her perpetrator, she met her husband, Lee. It was also her thirtieth birthday.

In 1999, Norris was diagnosed with PTSD, but she didn't know what that was. As years went by she learned about it but didn't want to admit that she had it. "I'm such a fighter," she said. Also hindering her ability to get help was the even greater need to protect her military career. Reporting sexual assault sends out red flags to the chain of command. "As soon as you ask for help, you lose your confidentiality," she said. "I didn't want to lose the ability to rise through the ranks. So I did the best I could."

That was also the same year Norris realized the military had little to offer for her acute stress. "I was blown away that the military had nothing to offer me after four different perps," she said.

Right after September 11, 2001, Norris's squadron deployed. The airmen had to report to duty the following weekend. She was living with her dad, who was dying of bone cancer. She left him Friday night, and soon after he shot himself. She found out the next day while on guard duty. "My dad was my rock," she said. "It was bad enough watching him die, but to lose him like that . . ."

This was his way of letting her go. She felt like she never got to say goodbye.

The suicide resulted in Norris getting assistance. While she definitely needed help for the rapes and sexual assaults, she first got aid because of the suicide. Getting help wouldn't be held against her if it were for her father's suicide. The same couldn't be said if she sought aid for the sexual attacks.

She started taking medication. You can't transfer to another squadron or deploy if you're on medication. Everyone in the squadron knew about the suicide. Her commander made her non-deployable. In October 2001, her squadron deployed without her. She deployed on a short temporary duty (TDY) assignment to Saudi Arabia in November 2001 in support of Operation Southern Watch but never got sent to Iraq or Afghanistan with the unit. However, she worked for them at the squadron and still felt like she was contributing.

When necessary, she trained herself. "I totally kicked ass," she said. She created standing operation procedures for new communications equipment that arrived with no directions. Then she trained everyone else on the equipment. She eventually became the team chief for the satellite communications team.

When the squadron returned from deployment, morale was low. There was a mass exodus of airmen leaving the guard. Norris asked to be transferred back to Maine because it was a long four-hour drive to Massachusetts. Sometimes she would have to pull over and sleep on the side of the road. Because she was in a critical position she was stop-loss, which meant she could not leave her current position in satellite communications. When the stop-loss was over, they wouldn't let her go because she was the subject-matter expert and had been an effective trainer. But they also wouldn't promote her because she didn't have leadership skills. Since the mass exodus included her shop, she was the only one left who was qualified to take the team chief position. She eventually received her technical sergeant stripe.

In 2005, Norris got transferred back to Maine and changed career fields to something that would be safer for women. Emergency management was her new career. She also earned a master's degree in public policy and management.

A year later Norris's PTSD was compounded from drinking alcohol again, so she quit and recommitted to her husband, Lee, who was active duty in the Air Force. They had met in 2001 and he wanted to get married at the time, but it wasn't until 2005 that she was ready for him. Before then, she didn't trust anybody, let alone a man.

She and Lee moved to McChord AFB in Washington State for a few months. Her PTSD was triggered when she learned about

Suzanne Swift, an Army soldier who refused to deploy to Iraq with her perpetrator. When Swift went public in the Washington newspapers, it was the first time Norris had seen military sexual assault discussed. She was inspired by someone speaking out publicly—in a newspaper. She eventually learned she could get help from the VA for military sexual trauma. She was still having headaches and physical symptoms.

In 2007, Norris's counselor had her write out her story as she saw it, which included blaming herself for going to the recruiter's home. Then she wrote the story again with a different mindset. This time the rape wasn't her fault. She was the victim of a calculated crime.

As she worked through the rape by the recruiter, Norris wanted to get as healthy as possible as quickly as possible using the free services of the VA. She went to counseling, group therapy, seminars, and workshops on PTSD and mindfulness. She tried to go inpatient in New York but only lasted two of the five weeks because she didn't like being away from home for so long. She couldn't handle being somewhere where she didn't know anyone. The most difficult part of her recovery was not feeling safe, and feeling vulnerable when by herself. She could control her environment at home.

A good deal of Norris's healing has been through advocacy, first for herself and then for others.

Fortunately, she had studied social work at a university after graduating from high school. In doing so, she learned about herself and different coping skills. She was resourceful from the start. When bad things happened to her, she knew she couldn't get by on her own, so she reached out to others.

In 1999, Norris had realized there were no health services for a woman who had been sexually assaulted in the military (she had to pay out of her pocket for counseling relating to retaliation). In 2007, when she found out she was losing her career because she was getting help for crimes perpetrated against her in the line of duty, she stepped up her advocacy a notch. She was being medically discharged for PTSD after fourteen years in the Air Force. This was the beginning of the end of her career.

Norris had to fill out a pre-deployment form and write on it that she was taking an antidepressant. She didn't realize at the time that if she went to the VA for the onset of PTSD, she would lose her career. After filling out the form, she was kicked off base and told she couldn't return to work without permission from her doctor. "Once you are deemed non-deployable, you are deemed useless," Norris said.

In hindsight, Norris realizes the VA was right in preventing her from deploying. They told her that if anything happened to her in Iraq, she probably would not have survived because of her PTSD. It is still so bad that if anyone comes near her uninvited, she blacks out. She didn't understand when the VA told her she couldn't deploy, but she gets it now. So she gave into the fact that her career was over and began fighting for her military retirement.

She contacted Sen. Olympia Snowe of Maine. "I will always be thankful for her," Norris said. "She helped me get the retirement I deserved." Norris could have tried to save her career in the Air Force, but she was so broken from reporting the crimes that she decided not to fight back this time and to get out. She realized that not being in the military was healthier for her.

Predators don't discriminate. They're opportunists. They don't care about gender or age. They go for the weakest and most vulnerable. Norris had been young and naïve and usually one of a few women in all three of her squadrons. They were banking on the fact that she wasn't going to report.

Norris said her healing is never ending. "I continuously work on the next thing that pops up. I either have to accept the way things are or find tools that will help me work through the issues. If I had let negative things take me down, I would have been gone a long time ago. I like to turn negatives into positives . . . how does this make me a better person and make me stronger?"

When she saw that sexual assaults, bullying, and ostracizing were affecting her ability to cope, it also helped her healing. She started individual counseling, where she spent time talking about how she had been shamed into silence. She had become so withdrawn. "I had to take my mindset and change it," she said. "Take away the shame that I was wrong. Others thought I must have done something wrong and asked for it."

She has accepted that she did nothing wrong and believes strongly that the perpetrators should be the ones who are blamed and shamed.

In the fall of 2011, she started advocating for an organization that helps victims of military sexual assault and harassment. She was motivated by the knowledge that the PTSD and anxiety were preventing her from being all she could be. She wanted to use her master's degree, yet she couldn't work in environments where men were in charge, controlling her. She asked herself: Having PTSD, what can I do that is fulfilling but in which I can control when and where I go to work?

Volunteering was the answer. She was well versed in how both the military and the VA handled victims with military sexual trauma "If I don't do this, I'll feel like I'm dying inside," she said. "That I don't have any purpose."

Becoming an advocate got her invited to testify before Congress. She spoke to the House Armed Services Committee. She told them that people aren't reporting because of retaliation. She told her story of being sexually assaulted not once, twice, or three times—but four times.

"Here you go, Congress," she said. "This is how the military treated me after reporting four perpetrators, and now I have compounded PTSD."

She continues to work with victims every day. She advocates for them and connects them to the appropriate resources and referrals. One of the most rewarding cases Norris has worked on was helping a female airman who had been gang-raped get justice. The woman feared for her life. She was denied an expedited transfer in the Air Force. Norris was livid. She contacted people. Because of the hard work of Norris and others, they were able to get the female airman away from that base and eventually out of the military. She was a success story because she had a mom who loved her and wouldn't let them condone the rape. She received retirement benefits. "They were trying to kick her out for being bipolar," Norris said, adding sarcastically, "Really? We've never heard that before. It was a stressful case but paid off in the long run." It was a common tactic of the VA to diminish complaints of men and women to personality disorders or adjustment disorder.

In 2013, at the suggestion of a friend, Norris went to Ponte Vedra Beach, Florida, to get a service dog. Norris was skeptical. She never had a dog of her own because she thought it would be overwhelming. Yet she and Onyx, a black lab, instantly hit it off.

"I never imagined in a million years that a dog could change my entire existence," she said. Norris couldn't walk outside without taking an anxiety pill. Now she just takes Onyx with her everywhere she goes. "It's like having my own personal bodyguard," she said. The dog has her back. She's already saved Norris from a couple of unruly characters.

Onyx is part of her routine. Norris's anxiety used to get the best of her. Now she gets up, plays with Onyx, feeds her, walks her.

"She makes me smile," Norris said. "She loves me. The closer we get, the more of a bond we create. I was all shut down."

Onyx is even helping Norris with her relationship with her husband. The dog is showing her how to release anxiety. Norris can now enjoy more and appreciate more. She feels the change not just in her mind but also in her body. In situations where Norris in the past would have had a meltdown, she finds that Onyx is distracting her.

During one nightmare, she awoke to Onyx cuddled up beside her as if to say, "It's okay. You're safe."

"Even in my sleep she's got my back," Norris said.

Advocacy has given Norris a voice to speak up, not only for herself but for others. And Onyx has given Norris the strength to walk without fear and to go to veterans' retreats and treatment programs to get more help for PTSD.

Norris still struggles with PTSD, but now she can see the light at the end of the tunnel. For years she fought suicide on a daily basis. She had a gun that she eventually gave away because it was too dangerous for her to have around the house. Now she is thankful she never followed through with those thoughts. Those were the days she couldn't see the light at the end of the tunnel. The light started with Lee helping her. She wanted to get well and return his kindness. Then came Onyx. She also helped her to love again and gave her the courage to go out, seek help, and be resourceful.

Now Norris maintains a website, militaryjusticeforall.com, to help other MST victims. It is dedicated to those who have lost their lives through homicide and suicide. She also has two blogs, jennifernorris and PTSD. She can do all the writing and research she wants from the comfort of her home.

The bottom line?

"MST is as bad as we're saying, and we're not prey."

The Artful Warrior and Her Veterans

Tech Sgt. Vera Roddy

IT WAS THE YEAR 2000 WHEN GULF WAR VETERAN VERA RODDY realized that the Wisconsin veterans were "her" veterans.

She was a case manager for a service provider for veterans. Her job was to work with homeless veterans and their families. She specialized in veterans with service-connected disabilities who couldn't go back to school or work. One of her philosophies was, "There but for the grace of God go I."

As a Gulf War veteran, she believes she could have easily slipped into homelessness when she returned home. Instead, when she got laid off from a job, everything fell into place for her. She felt that God was looking out for her. Now it was her turn to look out for veterans.

Roddy is a confident, articulate, and connected woman. She is a divorced mother of two who lives in Milwaukee. She loves veterans and will do most anything for them. She is happily immersed in the veteran community, attending VFW meetings and fish fries on a regular basis with an entourage of other vets who are often women, but not always.

In 1975, Roddy married an airman; two years later, at the age of twenty, she joined the Air Force. She traveled to Germany, where she became an aircraft subsystems mechanic when the Air Force first opened nontraditional careers to women. Roddy left active duty in 1981 and joined the reserves. In 1982, her daughter Anneliese was born at Bitburg Air Base in Germany. Roddy returned to Wisconsin, where she started college. During this period she took a class on psychology, fell in love with the subject, and changed her major from business to psychology.

Roddy became a nearly full-time reservist at Kelly Air Force Base in San Antonio, Texas. There she worked in an aircraft battle-damage repair squadron, where she worked in inventory management and as a training manager. Her son Michael was born at Wilford Hall Medical Center on Lackland Air Force Base in San Antonio.

In 1987, her husband was sent to Milwaukee as a recruiter and Roddy became a weekend warrior, working for the Air Force two weeks during the fiscal year and one weekend a month. That's when she also became a mental health technician, but because of military downsizing she lost her reserve job in Milwaukee. She traveled to Chicago instead, where she worked in aeromedical evacuation for the medical services support squadron. While she was away, her mom watched her children.

In 1991, Roddy was activated for Operation Desert Storm. She deployed to Riyadh, Saudi Arabia, where she was sent to King Khalid Military City (KKMC), 35 miles from the Iraq border. Roddy was there for almost three months as a mental health technician at the 1st Tactical Aeromedical Staging Facility (Provisional) and provided medical and mental health care to anyone with psychiatric injuries such as depression, PTSD, schizophrenia, suicidal ideation, and other illnesses that made them unfit to return to duty.

It was here that she also learned how to provide amputee care, burn care, postsurgical care, and most importantly care to those who survived friendly fire. Roddy had excellent medics as trainers. Because of her civilian employment in physical medicine and rehabilitation, she got the opportunity to do "talk therapy" (another name for psychotherapy) about what post-injury life would be like for her patients as she provided their medical care.

Everyone that goes to war seems to have an "aha!" moment. Roddy's came in January 1991 when a helicopter pilot came in on a litter. He had been shot down and forced to make a hard crash. The pilot suffered a major brain injury and was in a medically induced coma and on life support. Seeing the patient made it clear to Roddy that she was at war. "That stopped me dead in my tracks," she said. "If we do nothing, that boy will surely die."

To Roddy, the war became like a bad movie, often in slow motion. Sometimes she felt a part of it; at other times she felt remote and disengaged from it. Anybody who joins the military knows that war is a possibility, but few think it's going to happen to them, Roddy said. Especially when she signed up at the end of the Cold War, during a time of relative peace, and was a reservist. When the war ended, Roddy was in the first group of airmen released to go home. She still remembers missing her son's fifth birthday by four days. He was home with Roddy's mom.

Back in the desert in 1991, Roddy began to realize she was ill. Her symptoms included constant pain to the tailbone, right sacroiliac joint, hip, and shoulder, as well as fatigue and memory problems. She liked to walk but found that she could no longer walk long distances. She did the 20K Volksmarch walks in Germany from 1978 to 1981 without a problem. Now she couldn't walk from one building to the next without getting winded. Even worse, her once-sharp memory turned foggy.

After returning to her reserve unit in Chicago, Roddy was placed on medical hold for five months for what eventually became known as Gulf War illness (chronic multisymptom illness), although it was undiagnosed at the time. Her medical records were reviewed by Headquarters Air Force Reserves in Macon, Georgia, because several reserve units were reporting members returning with a mysterious unknown illness. Next thing she knew, she was discharged from the military, not medically but due to military spending cutbacks.

Her worst days were when she first returned from the war. She was working full-time in her civilian job while also a reservist, a mom, and a part-time student. That was a heavy burden under the best of circumstances. Meanwhile, she still suffered from the mysterious ailment that had begun afflicting her in the desert. On her worst days, which were every several weeks, she'd crash and couldn't get out of bed. Even going to the bathroom was a chore.

Depression and anxiety were ruled out. She worked in a psychology clinic with more than twenty psychologists and social workers who were trained to make a mental health diagnosis. "I think one of my coworkers would have said to me, 'Vera, you need to do something about this,' but no one ever did." They all recognized the physical symptoms she was dealing with. She worked with these people before and after deployment.

In February 1991, Roddy knew something was wrong and sought medical care. Before that, she never even got a cold. In July 1992 she opted not to reenlist because she was too sick. She always thought she'd go back and finish her enlistment, but she never did. She was an E6 (technical sergeant) when she got out. Nevertheless, in 1991 she earned an associate of arts degree from the University of Wisconsin–Waukesha. Her illness slowed her down physically but not mentally, and she was all for pursuing an education. She worked during the daytime and went to school at night.

There's another saying that Roddy likes: "'Use it or lose it.' If you don't use your mind, you will lose it," she said. She is curious

by nature. Since finishing her formal education, she has continued to take adult enrichment classes in everything from art to
trauma counseling.

With the military behind her, Roddy settled back into being
a mom and an employee in physical medicine and rehab while
pursuing her service-connected disability. Her divorce followed
in 1995. It took ten years to get 100 percent disability. Roddy was
one of the first 200 people on the Gulf War illness registry. She
received incremental increases in disability over a decade, starting with a 0 rating in 1992. On a Friday in 1997, she found out she
was 70 percent service-connected, or disabled; on the following
Monday, she got a pink slip at her civilian job, along with the rest
of her department. Roddy finished her last year of college, earning a bachelor's degree in psychology, under vocational rehab.
People say, "Vera, I don't know how you do it. You always land on
your feet." If she hadn't received the disability, she wouldn't have
been able to support herself and her children. She worked with
homeless veterans and knows how close she came to being one
of them. "There but for the grace of God go I" continued to be
her personal mantra.

In 2000 she became a case manager for the Center for Veterans Issues, a service provider for veterans who are at risk of
becoming homeless. That's when she really went to work for
veterans. That's when she started calling them "my vets." She
worked with homeless veterans and their families. Each case was
unique, from drug abusers to women who had prostituted themselves. Some were left homeless because of family situations. One
situation that came to mind was a woman who left the job market
to take care of her mother. When the mother died, she gave all
her money to her son, leaving the daughter penniless. Some were
eligible for benefits but didn't know it. Roddy helped them with
that. All were vets, and they all came from a place of success in the

military. Her philosophy was to go back to that original success and build on it. "They gained a pride in their veteran status that they didn't have before meeting me," she said.

Roddy recalls one veteran who was over fifty-five and a chronic alcoholic. She helped him access veteran's benefits and get into a twelve-step program. He also started volunteering and helping other vets. When she sees him in the community, they hug. He's clean and sober and has had his own apartment for a number of years. She opened his eyes to the possibilities, and he did the rest.

On 9/11, Roddy was admitted to the VA for a cellulitis infection on her leg. As she watched with one eye on the nurse's station and the other on the television, she observed nurses clearing out beds for potential patients from one of the crash sites. Having worked Air Evac in the military, she knew the hospital was part of the national emergency health care system. By 1 P.M., she had been discharged. She remembers feeling a sense of urgency to get back to her job to make sure her vets were ok. And she needed to get home to make sure her children were all right. Since the attacks were military related and she already had deployed once, she knew they would be worried that she would deploy again. All federal facilities were on lockdown. Roddy had to receive special permission to have her daughter visit her in the hospital. Her son, Mike, was in gym class. They had gotten a TV and turned it on. Roddy called the school and had the principal pull him out of class so she could let her son know she was ok.

In March 2002, all of Roddy's physical symptoms worsened to the degree that she applied for 100 percent disability. She quit her job and went to the Disabled American Veterans (DAV) service office, which held her power of attorney, to pursue service-connected disability on her behalf and to report her need for an increase in service-connected compensation as soon as possible. In October 2002, she rated 100 percent disabled. During the process, she used up all her savings but never missed a mortgage payment.

So, what did Roddy need healing from? Musculoskeletal issues, chronic fatigue and pain, fibromyalgia, memory problems, and gastrointestinal issues, all of which are presumed to be service-connected. If you didn't have those problems prior to deployment and you went to the first Persian Gulf War, you're presumed to have Gulf War illness. There is still very little known about the illness, which adds to the frustration. "I think that's what I needed healing from—the unknown," Roddy said. "I also needed to still feel like I was a useful member of society. Because what do you do when you're thirty-three years old and you come back from war and can't work in a society that expects you to work until you are sixty-five or seventy?"

One illness can be difficult to deal with. Roddy had multiple issues and diseases. Part of her recovery included recognizing that she could be a good employee, whether compensated or uncompensated, even if she couldn't punch a time clock. "I could still be productive, but I had to be productive at 2:30 in the morning sometimes," she said. "I found ways to make myself valuable to the veterans community by doing things as simple as typing up minutes from a meeting and sending emails at 2:30 in the morning."

Roddy describes herself as an all-or-nothing person. She likes to jump in with both feet and learn everything she possibly can about a job. When she was studying psychology, she took every psychology class possible. She also learned from people who were already in the field. "I read widely on my own, checking out books from the library and buying books on psychology. So I developed a specialty in that, and it paid off immeasurably in my career."

As a volunteer, she does the same thing with the veterans community. She wants to know every resource that is out there for veterans. And she doesn't just want to know about them—she wants to know that they are quality resources. Roddy likes to have firsthand knowledge of the resources available; this makes it easier to recommend various options and encourage a level of trust between the provider and recipient.

The physical challenges are not as easy to cope with. They affect Roddy on a daily basis. Having worked in physical medicine and rehabilitation, she learned from her patients that you're not disabled but "differently-abled." She remembers having a discussion with a woman who had multiple sclerosis and had two children at home. She lived in a two-level house. To go back and forth, the woman would crawl up the stairs or sit on her bottom and slide downstairs. That's one way she coped. "That always stuck with me." Roddy said. "So as I became more disabled, I found different ways to do things. . . . I still do everything I want to do, I just do them differently."

For instance, her friend Jen, also a vet, can't drive a car but can ride a bicycle. Roddy can't ride a bike but can drive a car. When Jen participates in a bike race, Roddy will drive her to and from the event and cheer her on. Sometimes they camp out overnight in Roddy's van. Together, they are a formidable team. "So am I still participating in the broader world?" she asked. "Yeah, absolutely. Do I get great joy out of it? You bet! But I have to do it differently."

There is a diagnosis in the *Diagnostic and Statistical Manual of Mental Disorders* for psychological factors affecting physical conditions. With any physical disability, a mental component could go along with it. Depression is a symptom affecting a small percentage of disabled veterans. "Do I fight hard not to slip into a depression?" Roddy asked. "I don't know. I don't think I've ever really been depressed. I don't want to go there if I don't have to. So I fight against that."

She still gets anxious about doing anything physically demanding. For instance, if she is alone and has to shovel snow, that is cause for anxiety. Roddy expects herself to assess what she can do and what she can't do, and to do the things she can. She also wrestles with what is good for her and what is challenging. What is enough, and what will leave her so debilitated that it will take her weeks to recover?

The physical demands of her disability always shadow her. "It's every waking moment of my daily life. I just choose not to focus on it. And again, it's something I learned working in a pain management clinic. So I practice a lot of things that I used to teach," she said. She understands that "when you're in pain, it's like a shadow on a sunny day. If you turn around and look at the shadow, you are conscious that it's there, but if you don't look around, you don't really know that it's there. It's not in the forefront of your awareness." Roddy makes a point of looking away from the shadows.

Assisting vets helps Roddy "immeasurably." It makes her feel good when she encourages her veterans to turn around and reach out to help the next veteran and they do it. "It's a hand up and not a hand out," she said. "I don't think anyone really wants to be dependent on a system, but we all need to be interdependent. It really boils down to veterans caring for veterans."

Roddy attributes her success with veterans to having great mentors who helped her find her way, people like World War II women veterans and Vietnam veterans. She was also mentored by a group of women over forty who had multiple sclerosis, a group she used to facilitate. Despite their disabilities, those ladies could do anything, she said. They had to plan a little more. They had to factor in their energy levels a little more. "When I was in Desert Storm, I thought if they could deal with what they were dealing with, I could deal with anything," Roddy said. "They were some of my strongest supporters before I went to war, while I was there, and after I came back." Those ladies were the ones who encouraged Roddy to pursue an MS diagnosis even though ultimately that wasn't it. It's because of their experiences that she found support in pursuing her own diagnosis, the still-mysterious Gulf War illness.

Roddy describes herself as "super resilient. I have all the best attributes of resiliency, so I'm blessed that way." In the military they call it "intestinal fortitude." She has a supportive family and community. She triumphs over adversity, is even-keeled, and doesn't get inappropriately angry at the system. Rather, she uses the system to the best of her ability and advantage.

But how does she deal with healing as a process, as something that doesn't occur overnight but that has to be dealt with day in and day out for the rest of her life? First you have to recognize that you need healing, she said. And then you have to look for sources of healing, which she believes are internal. "I think we all have the ability to heal ourselves," Roddy said.

Everyone deals or doesn't deal with healing as they age. It's part of the aging process. What's different for Roddy is that she had to learn to start healing at the age of thirty-three, which has taught her a lot about herself in the process. One thing she's learned is that she has "exceptional leadership skills." What she does in the veterans community isn't as much about resource management and getting people connected with their benefits as it is about leadership and platoons. "I've learned that every veteran needs a platoon, and every platoon needs a mission," she said.

She exercised a lot of that leadership ability legislatively and by helping to rally the women's veterans movement in Wisconsin. After women veterans started to hear the "band of sisters" moniker, around 2006, they realized the need for a supportive women veterans group. Men have a natural bond with one another, but suddenly there were all these women returning from war and they needed support. Roddy and other Wisconsin women vets tossed around some ideas and talked to other organizations to see what they could do for this generation of veterans who were coming home and were motivated and galvanized to do something. They needed to direct these new veterans.

"I think the camaraderie is the biggest factor," Roddy said. There are so many women in communities throughout this country that may not know another female veteran. "So if you can bring them together under any one umbrella, they are no longer alone," she said. "Each woman has her own unique story, but she has to realize that within the women's veteran community, she is more normal than abnormal."

One beauty of the veteran community, male or female, is that it crosses generations and branches. For instance, female veterans from World War II interact with women from the wars in Iraq and Afghanistan. World War II vets were Roddy's mentors. They opened many doors for her and told her which organizations to join.

Women veterans don't have a lot of state and national organizations like men have. Only a few have congressional charters, such as WAVES National, the Women Marines Association, the Women's Army Corps Association, and the Women in the Air Force Association. Traditional male organizations such as the VFW, AMVETS, the American Legion, and Disabled American Veterans are all open to women. The majority of their members are still male, however, which can be intimidating for a young female vet. On the other hand, some women who have joined these organizations have made lifetime friends with the men.

Roddy went to DAV Chapter 1 meetings every month for a year. Each time a member would direct her to the Auxiliary meeting room. Even after she explained she was a veteran, they would say, "But the Auxiliary meets over there." She quit going.

Of all the veterans service organizations she joined, she thought she would get the most resistance from the VFW. Quite the contrary: The members of the Gross-Yaksh Post 6498 in Wauwatosa, Wisconsin, welcomed her like their long-lost daughter.

Roddy met the women's veterans coordinator, Gundel "Gundy" Metz, and they forged a valuable professional and then personal relationship. Out of that relationship grew the Wisconsin women's veterans conference, which ran for about five years. The conference became their state convention and gave the female veterans a unified voice. It allowed them to meet their sisters in arms and find out what was going on with issues that affect women veterans.

Besides serving in the military, Roddy has racked up countless hours volunteering for veterans. For more than a decade she and her family served veterans food during the holidays at Vets Place Central, a residential transitional housing program.

In 2010 Roddy's life took another turn, this time for the better. She began following the story of Bob Curry, a Vietnam veteran who wanted vets to have an alternative to the bar scene as a place to hang out together. He came up with coffee shops as safe places for vets to socialize. Curry opened Dryhootch on Brady Street in Milwaukee in October 2011. The Dryhootch is a nonprofit organization that helps veterans and their families with a variety of integration issues, including PTSD, drug/alcohol addiction, and family support.

Roddy started one of the first peer mentor groups at the Dryhootch. The group is now called The Artful Warriors, but it is not really about art. They use creative arts to engage vets in a way traditional intervention might not reach someone who is in a safe environment yet still needs help, encouragement, or just friendship. Roddy has a knack for both art and bringing people together, so this type of volunteering is perfect for her. She began with *Wreck This Journal* by Keri Smith, a journal that prompts the reader to engage in different activities with the book. Three of the veterans had their own journals, and then someone bought more and donated them to the group.

Roddy said Artful Warriors is more about the camaraderie, sharing stories, and creating a new platoon and mission. The group meets every Tuesday from 11 A.M. to 3 P.M. The men and women range from poets and painters to jewelry makers and musicians. They represent vets who served in Vietnam through veterans from the wars in Iraq and Afghanistan.

The Artful Warrior provides an outlet for veterans to express themselves. People who never thought about writing now want to write their story or express it in poetry. It also offers the veterans an opportunity to get out of the house and socialize on a regular basis.

Like Roddy said, it's about the art, but it's more about the veteran. Kevin Hough can attest to this. An airman, he returned to the Milwaukee area after being gone for some years. "Without Vera, I'd have no contacts in the Milwaukee veteran community," he said. "She's a map. She helps me navigate the myriad of programs and people. She's done the legwork already. She's giving back. She inspires me to want to do that."

Tegan Griffith (see page 31), who served in the Marine Corps, said Roddy took her under her wing. "It's huge when you have supporters like Vera behind you," she said. "She's encouraging. If a vet presents herself to Vera, she helps them. She has a built-in networking skill."

Roddy served on the Wisconsin Department of VA Women's Veterans Committee, a two-year appointment. Griffith came onto the committee as Roddy's term was expiring. "She was our mentor on the committee," Griffith said. "You have to be fresh off the press to not meet Vera in Wisconsin. She's protective of her vets. Once you're in the Vera club, you're golden."

Helping Others Find Their Way

Sister Sarge

LINDA MCCLENAHAN, AKA SISTER SARGE, REMEMBERS VISITING the Vietnam Veterans Memorial and searching for the names of soldiers she knew. She looked at the rows and rows of names. Then she looked at the people pointing to the names, and the flowers and boots carefully placed on the ground below them. It was too much.

The next thing she knew, she was hugging a soldier dressed in military fatigues. When she came up for air, she thanked the stranger. He said, "Not a problem, sister veteran. Just pass it on." That same night she passed it on by hugging another crying vet.

Born in Minnesota in 1949, McClenahan's family moved to the San Francisco Bay Area when she was five. There she went through twelve years of Catholic school. When she graduated, she planned to become a nun. But life had other plans for her.

She grew up in Berkeley in the 1960s, a time and location fraught with protests and violence. An intelligent young woman, McClenahan wasn't about to rely on people in the street telling her what to think of the war. She wanted to find out for herself. So at the age of eighteen, she joined the Women's Army Corps. It was 1967. Two years later, she shipped out to Long Binh, Vietnam, where she served from November 1969 to November 1970. "It sounds like a year, but it was actually a lifetime," she said.

She worked in communications at the service desk, check control, and cryptography. At the service desk, she received messages. If a message came in garbled, she would send it back and ask for a repeat. She'd do the same if a message was incomplete. She would also respond to messages. At check control, she would patch one line into another so different parties could communicate. In cryptography, the code machines had to be reset every day so no one could figure out the outgoing and incoming messages. There were twenty-six small wires, and each had to go into a different hole so that messages coming across secure lines were readable. She reset the code machines by moving the wires into different holes in different combinations each day.

Working in cryptography gave McClenahan high-level clearance. She knew when a new general had orders because they came over in code. When dignitaries such as Bob Hope visited, the logistics were sent to McClenahan encoded because if the enemy knew about the large gathering, it would make the soldiers an easy target. Because of her clearance, McClenahan also had all the instructions for what to do if the area were overrun. She knew what to do with the grenade in the safe, how to destroy things and get out.

She worked twelve-hour shifts, from 6 A.M. to 6 P.M. or from 6 P.M. to 6 A.M., usually six days a week. During a couple of long pushes, no one got time off. She asked for Sundays off to go to church until she stopped believing in God.

In the command center were forty male soldiers and two other female soldiers. McClenahan is still friends with one of the

women, Gail. The guys were great, she said. They were like brothers and all hardworking. McClenahan was less fond of the guys in
the maintenance room, who had pin-ups of women. She usually
went to the 44th signal area to eat with the guys; otherwise, she
ate at the 24th evac hospital.

One day she went to an infantry unit party even though she
didn't really feel like going out. On the way back, a male soldier
got hit by sniper fire. McClenahan returned fire with an M16 that
had fallen to her feet when the soldier who had been holding it
was shot. The soldiers behind her also returned fire. One of their
shots killed the sniper. McClenahan realized in that moment that
she could take a life and not think twice about it.

Another time McClenahan and female soldier Adrianne
Shamp were on a bus headed to the 24th evac mess hall. The
driver of the bus was new, as were several of the soldiers on the
bus. Medevac helicopters started arriving up ahead, but the bus
driver wasn't stopping. McClenahan and Shamp rushed to the
front of the bus. McClenahan slammed her foot on the brake
while Shamp yelled at the driver. "You stop for the wounded!"
she demanded.

When she got out of the bus, McClenahan saw a patient who
had been stripped of his clothes and was burned from head to
toe. It looked as though he was 100 percent burned, she said.
"The smell was something I'll never forget. The way he looked.
The way the medics looked running with him and an IV." The
image is very deep. He looked like he was eighteen or nineteen.

After the area was cleared, they proceeded in the bus to the
mess hall. Shamp and McClenahan were the only ones from the
bus who felt like eating. Others had turned white as ghosts; some
were vomiting.

McClenahan dreamed about this soldier for years. This incident was one of many times when she had to "suck it up" and

move on. "We, like so many of the men and women, learned quickly to stuff all feelings to protect ourselves," she said. "We had to eat, so we did. In Vietnam there was an expression, 'Don't mean a thing.' Years later I realized that I was either in that mode or 'In order to make anything mean anything, I had to make everything mean everything.' So I was either numb or overreacting."

A trauma McClenahan wouldn't discuss has to do with an orphanage. She explained that every unit adopted an orphanage, whose kids they fed and clothed. But there was a situation. She sums up her Vietnam experience by saying it wasn't supposed to be like that. The smell. The good guys versus bad guys.

After a series of traumas that included being gang-raped, McClenahan no longer believed in God and had fragmented into another person. The naïve, sweet, patriotic young woman no longer existed. She went over as Linda and came back as Lin, a tough old Army sergeant who wouldn't take shit from anyone and who was a drunk. Some friends still call her Lin; when she hears that name, she knows what era the friend is from.

When she returned home, McClenahan was having physical problems that her family doctor thought might be malaria. She was sent to the VA in Martinez, California. She had to convince them she was a veteran. The doctor asked her if she made good money there, "whoring around." It was 1971.

She was in the reserves from 1970 to 1976. At that time, she was no longer interested in becoming a nun. She didn't believe in God or the military, or in anything else for that matter. She was trying to find out where she fit in because she didn't feel like she fit anywhere.

While in the reserves, McClenahan went to work in telecommunications for Bechtel Corporation for fifteen years. The company reminded her a little of the military because it had offices all over the world. Still angry, McClenahan would get into trouble at times for being too intense and too much of a perfectionist. She was told that the things she got angry at were legitimate but that her anger was extreme. "I seemed angry all the time," she said. Trivial things, such as a pickup softball game, meant a lot.

During her tenure at Bechtel, McClenahan came up with plans to revamp the company's communication plan and save it $350,000. The plan ended up saving Bechtel even more. But McClenahan left the company after a reorganization of the communications department. Fortunately, she had earned a degree in business administration with a minor in psychology while working for the company.

She was offered a job by a good friend of twenty years to coach the Immaculate Conception Academy's first softball team in San Francisco, and she began teaching physical education at the academy. She also worked part-time as an assistant custodian at her apartment complex.

While McClenahan was still working for Bechtel, Vietnam veterans in California were commissioned to help build a Vietnam memorial at the state capitol in Sacramento. They wanted a woman to be part of the commission. McClenahan led the commission. It's the first Vietnam veterans memorial that acknowledged her and other women. She is one of the bronze characters.

The experience of working on the memorial was healing. McClenahan and others went through thousands of pictures to find just the right memorial and they ran a serious fundraising campaign. She met a lot of great people. She heard incredible stories and became part of something much larger than herself. "I was just an ordinary person who got caught up in an extraordinary thing," McClenahan said.

She vividly remembers one fundraising event for the memorial, a dance in Fresno, California. She befriended a veteran named Jim who was in a wheelchair. Later, as she was getting ready to leave the event, the DJ started playing her favorite song, "(I Can't Get No) Satisfaction" by the Rolling Stones. She couldn't leave. She danced with Jim. "He had that wheelchair spinning and wheeling," she said. "It was the best dance of my life."

Comedian Robin Williams helped the commission raise money, and Bob Hope was there when they broke ground. The memorial was dedicated in front of about 80,000 people in December 1988. As the chairman of the commission, McClenahan spoke.

While still teaching at Immaculate Conception Academy, McClenahan returned to the church. But she wasn't so sure about her future within the church—as a sister or a nun. She didn't think any convent in its right mind would want her after what she had been through. By this time she had decided there was a God, but she wasn't sure what that meant. She started church-hopping to find one that felt right. Nothing felt like a match, so she decided to figure out God without a church. The Catholic high school felt like her home. While walking with a priest one day, she asked him what she needed to do to get back into the church. The priest told her to go to confession and then to communion within twenty-four hours. It had been years since her last confession; she suggested the priest sit down.

During this period McClenahan also learned the difference between spirituality and religion. Spirituality is an individual relationship with God. It's a growing, living thing. Because God is alive, spirituality is alive. It's a relationship, and relationships are ever-changing. Religion is a set of rites, rituals, and traditions that a group of people believe in and use to worship the god of their common understanding. You can't grow in religion, but you can become more educated.

McClenahan started having conversations with a convent of sisters in Mission San José, California, but it wasn't a good fit.

Then one night she was correcting papers and listening to Harry Reasoner on *60 Minutes* when she saw a remarkable group of Dominican sisters from Mississippi. She sent a check and a letter to the sisters. In the letter back to her, she was connected with a sister from Racine, Wisconsin. McClenahan and the sister had additional contact. She was put in touch with the vocation director.

While Wisconsin seemed like quite a stretch from California, every day happenings pointed to the Midwest. She didn't have the money to visit Wisconsin and check it out. Yet the day after she talked with the vocation director, she received a check for $500 from someone who owed her money. McClenahan moved to Racine in 1992, twenty-two years after returning from Vietnam. Thankfully, she said, the sisters were more interested in where she was going than in where she had been. She joined the Sisters of St. Dominic of Racine, also known as the Racine Dominicans, in 1992. She took her first vows in 1995 and her final vows in 2000.

McClenahan earned a master's degree in social work and started counseling in the private sector, working mostly with trauma survivors and addicts. She took a job with a veterans assistance program and connected with the International Conference of War Veteran Ministers and their post-traumatic spiritual retreat.

She got involved with Mayslake Ministries in Lombard, Illinois. She offered to bring the post-traumatic spiritual retreat to them. "It's a real gift for me when people share the deepest parts of their lives," she said. "It's good for me to feel that I'm helping others begin or continue finding their path toward healing."

McClenahan realizes the retreats aren't a be-all and end-all for healing, but do provide another piece of the puzzle. They offer another way of looking at things. The retreats try to touch people at their heart and soul, tugging at something deeper. McClenahan runs four retreats a year. Part one is for initial post-traumatic spiritual issues, and part two is for people who are still dealing with trauma but want to deepen their relationship with God.

While working at the veterans assistance program, McClenahan brought part of the retreat program to traumatized vets and realized its effectiveness. She started modifying it and doing programs with vets and getting a positive reaction. It didn't matter what the trauma was: Trauma is trauma. But military trauma has its own unique lens, McClenahan said. For instance, military sexual trauma is often the experience of one soldier raping another. The people who are supposed to have your back betray you. It is incestuous. The retreats provide a safe, nonjudgmental environment.

McClenahan can run these retreats because she has been there. She speaks from personal experience. She believed in God but was madder than hell at God. She believed that if she did everything she was supposed to do, God would take care of her. That's what she grew up believing. She believed she had kept up her end of the bargain but that God hadn't. "I eventually realized that the God I no longer believed in was the God of my childhood," she said. McClenahan wasn't alone in her beliefs. A lot of veterans were uncertain about their relationship with God.

Somewhere along the way, McClenahan realized that God was present for her during the traumatic times. She revisited and figured out where God was and reconciled her relationship with God. "Wait," she said, "it's not reconciliation. It's all brand new and it keeps growing."

Throughout the years of working for Bechtel and then the high school, and then moving to Wisconsin, McClenahan has had to deal with her own skeletons from war. The emotional roller coaster of being a traumatized war veteran took its toll on her. Nothing went away when she returned to the United States. Life didn't get easier. The anger and rage from her traumatic experiences followed her home and gnawed at her.

When she was driving and got mad, McClenahan would tailgate the person who had just cut her off. She would break out in a sweat and feel her stomach in her throat. Now she has more choices. She is more likely to pull over and wait for her breathing to settle down.

"The road to healing is long, hard, messy, and incomplete," she said. One of her favorite scriptures is Psalm 38:8: "I am feeble and utterly crushed; I roar with anguished heart." She has done a lot of roaring and lashing out.

During her recovery, she has learned that anger is a secondary emotion. "It's a reaction to another emotion we feel, but anger seems better at the time," she explained. "It was more acceptable to be angry than to cry and show any sign of what I believed to be weakness."

She still has suicidal thoughts on her road to recovery. She is easily triggered by unexpected fireworks, people who try to intimidate her or walk up behind her, and by certain music. Music was very much a part of their lives in Vietnam. Songs such as "We've Gotta Get Out of This Place," "Satisfaction," "Abraham, Martin and John," and anything by Elvis are triggers that can send McClenahan right back to Vietnam.

The media is another trigger, especially when they compare natural disasters to a war zone: for instance, when they said Hurricane Katrina made the New Orleans area look like a war zone. "Too many things need to happen to make something a war zone," she said. "The only thing that looks like a war zone is a war zone. The only thing that smells like a war zone is a war zone."

She recalled being in group therapy with individuals who had PTSD. Someone mentioned that they were suicidal. The counselor asked, "Do you have a plan?" McClenahan exploded.

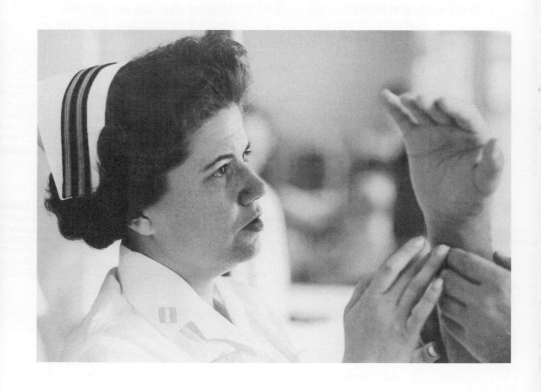

A Life of Service

CDR Barbara Miller

IN 2008, BARBARA ELLEN MILLER BECAME THE FIRST WOMAN TO be inducted into the Connecticut Veterans Hall of Fame. I found her in an independent retirement community in my hometown of Mystic, Connecticut.

"Independent" is the key word for this Navy nurse who served from 1962 to 1982. I asked Miller, who is eighty-one, how she happened to join the Navy.

"Everyone laughs when I tell the story," she said. It was the farthest thing from her mind. She had graduated from Keuka College in New York in 1956, worked for several years, and was finishing up her master's degree at the University of Maryland in Baltimore in 1961. "I didn't have two nickels to rub together," she said, recalling that every once in a while she and some other nurses would "sell our blood" to pay their parking lot fees. She had finished her classes and was writing her thesis. That summer she received several job offers to work in different areas of the country.

In September, she was packed and ready to leave Maryland. While walking down the street one day, she saw a big poster: "Join the Navy and See the World."

"I stood there and looked at it and said, 'You know, I could serve my country and that would really be great. I could travel and get paid for it. Now what better deal is there than that?'" So Miller went into the recruiting office, walked up to the counter, and said she wanted to join the Navy.

A young sailor looked at her and said, "Do you type?"

"Type?" she asked. "I don't type. I'm a nurse. Nurses don't type." At least they didn't back then, she said.

He told her to take the ladder to the second deck. She didn't see a ladder so she took the stairs, which led to a big room. There, behind a desk, sat a woman in a blue suit with "all kinds of gold stripes and buttons and a chest full of ribbons."

"May I help you?"

"Yes, Ma'am. I think I'd like to join the Navy. I'm a nurse."

The woman behind the desk opened her mouth and looked at Miller. "Are you sure?" she asked.

I'm almost thirty years old, Miller said to herself. *What's the matter with this lady?* "You've got a sign out on the sidewalk that says I can travel and serve my country," Miller said. It didn't say you'd get paid for it, but Miller thought you did.

She asked Miller if she was employed. Miller said she was finishing up her master's degree at the University of Maryland. "I work here and there," she said.

The female officer got up and put a big packet of papers on the table in front of Miller, asked her some questions, and the next thing Miller knew she was signing her life away.

She went back to the nurse's residence at the university. Everyone was coming out of their rooms, saying, "For crying out loud, Miller, where have you been? We want to go to supper. What have you been doing?"

"I just joined the Navy," she said.

"What, are you, crazy?" they asked.

"No, I don't think I'm crazy," Miller replied. "I think I made a good decision."

A few days later she drove to Beacon, New York, to her parents' house. One morning during her visit she decided to announce her decision about entering the Navy Nurse Corps to her mom and dad while having breakfast. "Dad thought I had made a 'good decision.' However, Mom wasn't so sure. She looked shocked and said, 'Good heavens, why did you do that? You won't like being ordered around, and you will be sent to some far-off corner of the world. What happened to the job offers you had in Washington, D.C., New York State, and Florida?'" She told her mom she thought it would be a great experience for both work and travel and that she would manage fine. During Miller's Navy career, her mom and dad enjoyed visiting her, seeing her apartment and the area where she lived, and meeting her friends.

In December 1961 Miller was sworn into the Navy in Washington, D.C., and a month later she reported to Officer Candidate School (OCS) in Newport, Rhode Island, where the snowbanks loomed over her head and the cold wind blew off Narragansett Bay. After OCS, she spent the next two years at National Naval Medical Center (NNMC) Bethesda in the VIP/ officer quarters. She cared for congressional members, foreign service officers, high-ranking military officers (Adm. Thomas C. Kinkaid and Adm. Hyman G. Rickover, for example), and Vice President Lyndon B. Johnson, and assisted with physical examinations for President John Kennedy, Atty. Gen. Robert Kennedy, and Sen. Edward Kennedy.

In July 1964, Lieutenant Miller traveled aboard a military sea transport service (MSTS) vessel on her way to U.S. Naval Hospital Yokosuka, Japan, with three other Navy nurses. When she arrived, she was met by the chief nurse and one of the supervisors on staff. The hospital census was about 100. Miller became the orthopedic charge nurse.

Five months later, on Christmas Eve 1964, the Brink Hotel (the bachelor officer quarters for the Nurse Corps) in Saigon was bombed and four nurses were wounded. The conflict increased, and more American forces arrived. "We heard we would be expanding the hospital census and admitting many of the wounded Marines, as Naval Hospital Yokosuka was the only hospital in the Far East to accommodate large numbers of casualties," Miller said. Yokosuka expanded from 100 to 800 patients in a matter of a week. All those patients were young Marines right off the battlefields, covered in mud and debris.

Initially Miller worked around the clock. The nurses would be sent back to their quarters to shower and rest but Miller, like the other nurses, had a difficult time settling down and sleeping. Their adrenaline was flowing. She would be sent back to the barracks any time of day or night, but sleep didn't come easily. "Somehow the Lord gives you strength and you keep on working," Miller said.

When they got through the initial surge of patients, the chief nurse was adamant about the nurses getting their rest. She finally made a schedule where they worked a six-day week with one day off. The nurses were told not to go near the hospital on their day off.

Orthopedics, where Miller worked, was the area with the highest influx of patients because of all the arm and leg wounds. She said many patients had limbs blown off; some had "Punji stick" (a booby-trapped stake) wounds to the feet, or the side of their face gone, or other multiple wounds to the abdomen and back. "And it just kept on and on and on."

The young men were frightened when they arrived at the hospital. "They came in with big eyes . . . staring," Miller said. "They were scared." She recalled one young Marine who, when he saw Miller, pulled his sheet up to his face. She said she wasn't going to hurt him. "I'm your nurse. I'm here to take care of you."

He said, "Your railroad tracks."

At first Miller had no idea what he was talking about, but then it dawned on her. On her collar were two bars representing her rank as a lieutenant. The Marine had never seen a woman officer and was petrified.

She asked another young fellow, seventeen, what she could get for him. He said a big glass of ice water and a Bugs Bunny comic book. "I took care of the ice water and called the Red Cross and said get your comic book cart and bring it down here, and make sure you have a Bugs Bunny comic book on it." Sure enough they did.

Seeing casualties every day can wear on someone. How did Miller deal with it? She said she kept a sense of humor. She would laugh at herself—at something she said or did. "I often opened my mouth when I shouldn't have," Miller said.

And she prayed a lot. "I think, at least for me, prayer is essential in my life," Miller said. This was especially true of being a nurse in Yokosuka, where they didn't always have a doctor available to tell them what to do. The doctors were working around the clock in the operating room. They'd go onto the wards, but not frequently, and the nurses couldn't get them on the phone, so they had to make a lot of their own decisions. "I prayed that I was doing the right thing," she said.

"I loved my duty," Miller said. "I loved everything about it. I loved what I was doing. I loved the country. I had time to get out and enjoy the culture." She ended up speaking Japanese and later served as an interpreter in San Diego in an emergency room. She put 7,500 miles on her red Chevy in Japan. She drove all over because no one else would drive. "I'd pile up the car with Navy nurses and off we went," she said. "We worked hard for long hours, but when we were off duty we played hard."

In early 1966, Miller was returning from off base one evening when she smelled a lot of smoke. Some of the nurses were coming out of the quarters saying, "The hospital is on fire." Miller was dressed in a pair of powder-blue jeans and a powder-blue sweatshirt, and her hair had just been styled in a Japanese shop in town.

She ran down the hill, over to the hospital, and went right to the orthopedic ward. "I knew I had a new young nurse from the States who was on duty from 3 to 11," she said. "I thought, 'Oh dear, she's all by herself with a couple of corpsmen.'" When Miller got to the nurse, she was frozen in place. "I could see the flames lapping up the windows behind the beds of the patients," Miller said. She told one of the corpsmen to take the nurse outside, which he did.

In the meantime, Miller grabbed a big, long pair of sheers that were chained to the wall next to a large roll of wrapping paper; the men used the shears and paper to wrap gifts to send home. Any other time if she had tried to pull them away from the wall they wouldn't have budged. "But I believe the Lord gives us superhuman strength when we need it, and I gave one big yank and they came off," she said.

There were fifty men on the ward and most were in traction—legs and arms. And they were howling: "Get me out of here. I got out of Nam. Don't let me burn up in here."

"Hang on," Miller replied. "I'm coming."

"You know in the military we all know what to do," Miller said. "We all have a job. No one was saying 'What do I do?'"

"Bite the bullet and hang on," Miller said. "This is going to hurt." She proceeded to cut all the strings and let their legs and arms down. The corpsmen then rolled the men off the beds, onto blankets, and twisted the ends and dragged them outside. When Miller finished cutting the strings, she did the same thing. She dropped each patient onto her knee, to the deck, and then pulled him out the door. Between the corpsmen and Miller, they got all their patients out of the hospital safely.

An electrical fire had started in the ceiling of the auditorium attached to the hospital. It began around 6:40 in the evening. Miller remembers the time because that's when they would get the patients ready to go to the auditorium for a 7:00 movie. "Thank God they weren't there yet," she said.

Hundreds of patients and staff got out safely and no one was injured. Miller had fifty in-bed patients on the first deck and semi-ambulatory patients on the second deck. They hobbled out on their own. Orthopedics moved to the naval base gym for the next few days. "We functioned," Miller said. "In the military you function anywhere."

Miller arrived in Japan in July 1964 and left in July 1966. She returned on a Navy ship to Oakland, California, to a hostile crowd. The Marines had eggs and tomatoes thrown at them, and so did the nurses. "Hippies they said they were. What are hippies?" Miller asked. She soon found out.

She traveled in uniform and was accosted in airports. She had eggs thrown at her in Dulles outside Washington, D.C. At Kennedy in New York, a group of long-haired men surrounded her while she was reading a book and called her all kinds of nasty things. Out of nowhere came a Navy chief and a Marine sergeant. They told the hippies to get lost, then each sat on one side of her and said they were going to stay with her until she departed.

On a flight from Dulles to Los Angeles, the woman sitting next to Miller asked her if she was a policewoman.

"No, I'm U.S. Navy Nurse Corps," Miller said, and went back to reading her book.

The woman asked the stewardess for a different seat. "I will not sit with this military woman," she said.

"I thought, *Boy, isn't that something?*" Miller said.

In San Diego, she guest-lectured in uniform at a junior college. "That was a bad experience because people were nasty," Miller said. After that, whenever she lectured at a college she carried her uniform in a garment bag and changed in a bathroom or faculty room. And she stopped traveling in uniform through airports. "That was the times we were living in," she said.

Now when they return home the military is greeted less harshly. "There was nothing for us," she said. "But you learn to just take one day at a time. I enjoy each day and I don't look back. Every day is a good day. I'm a very optimistic, realistic-type person, and I just shrug those things off."

Miller also describes herself as stoic. When she was little and skinned her knees, her mom would sit her down and tell her it was okay. She wiped Miller's tears away. "Isn't that better?" her mom asked. Professionally, she was taught not to show emotion around patients.

Another trait Miller was taught at a young age was to do for others. "The world doesn't revolve around you," her mother said. "It's not just you. It's what you can do for other people." This played out in church and in Girl Scouts.

"I guess it must have really hit home because I've had a life of service," Miller said. "And I'm still trying to serve others."

Dealing with the sick and wounded was her profession, and she had plenty of time to prepare for it with four and a half years of school, which included hospital experience comparable to the number of patient-care hours in a hospital school of nursing program. Before she even went to Japan, she worked evenings, nights, holidays, and weekends. A nurse once asked her if she had to work Thanksgiving. Miller said, "You're in the U.S. Navy Nurse Corps. You'll work twenty-four seven if you have to. Patients don't pick up their blankets at 3:00 on Friday afternoon and return Monday morning."

She learned to deal with trauma when she worked in the ER as a student nurse in upstate New York. It was farming country, and there would be terrible accidents with tractors tipping over. "It wasn't easy because I was frightened," she said. "I wanted to do the right thing." She attributes her success in nursing to great instructors and supervisors.

"This is life," Miller said. "And when I got overseas and saw war injuries I thought, 'This is war.'"

Miller traveled from Japan to San Diego, where she worked at Naval Hospital (Balboa) San Diego from 1966 to 1969. She was assigned first to neurology, where she took care of spinal cord injuries from Vietnam—paraplegics and quadriplegics. She then transferred to the in-service Education Department. In the surgical ICU, she cared for patients following chest, cardiac, brain, and spinal cord surgeries.

Next she happened upon a unique experience. She was called into the chief nurse's office. "I am giving you a very special assignment," the chief nurse told her. "You are going to be the 3–11 nurse for the USS *Pueblo* crew when they return here to San Diego. You won't have any days off. You will be under tight security, you'll eat at a private table in the mess hall, and you won't associate with other Nurse Corps officers or anyone else." She could go to her apartment to sleep.

The USS *Pueblo* was a communications ship, and at the time comm vessels were not armed, Miller said. The *Pueblo* was in the

Pacific, and North Korea attacked the ship because they claimed it was in their waters. The North Koreans boarded the vessel, killed one of the sailors, and took over the ship as some of the officers below tried to pitch secret documents overboard. All the men on the *Pueblo* were prisoners in North Korea for more than a year. When they were released, they were taken to South Korea before heading for California. They arrived Christmas Eve 1968. "This was my most memorable Christmas Eve ever—seeing the crew reunited with their family," Miller said.

Miller greeted these men and was their evening nurse for the duration of their thirty-plus days in the hospital. "They arrived debilitated," Miller said. "Some were very ill. Many had been beaten, and suffered physical and emotional trauma."

She had seen the commanding officer of the vessel, Lloyd M. "Pete" Bucher, in Yokosuka. He would visit the officers' club in 1963–64. Miller described him as having a "nice physique." In 1968, after being imprisoned for over a year, he arrived at the hospital in a bus. He was helped off the bus, and Miller saw an emaciated man wearing a commander's hat too big for his head. She knew it must be Bucher.

From San Diego, Miller went to Naval Hospital Philadelphia, where she was assigned to the amputee service. In 1969, Philadelphia was the East Coast center for the amputees from Vietnam. Here, several hundred amputee patients were spread over many wards—large physical and occupational therapy departments, and a prosthetics department. Patients, mostly Marines, were missing one or more limbs upon admission and remained at the hospital through the revisions of their stumps, physical therapy, and fittings for prosthesis. "Our patients stayed until the day they walked out with their final prosthesis and their uniform on," Miller said.

She stayed in Philadelphia for three and a half years, where she received the rank of lieutenant commander. She also worked in dependent service as the supervisor and as the staff detailer, preparing multiple duty schedules for Nurse Corps officers, hospital corpsmen, civilian RNs and LPNs, and ward attendants. Thus, she had to quickly learn federal civil service policies.

One day Miller had a visit from the first woman admiral of the Navy, a Navy nurse. Rear Adm. Alene Duerk was the director of the Navy Nurse Corps. She came to Philadelphia to talk Miller into working at the Naval Medical Research Institute in Bethesda. This was a hard pill for Miller to swallow because she loved clinical nursing.

"I said, 'Well, ma'am, I'm willing to do whatever needs to be done for the Nurse Corps, but I don't think I'm the person you want there.'"

Duerk said she needed clinical expertise in this area of research.

"'Yes, ma'am,' I said. And off I went to the Naval Medical Research Institute in Bethesda."

At the research institute, everyone took turns being officer of the day, which for Miller meant leaving her own department and going to the administration department to assume the watch from 4 P.M. to 8 A.M. Her duties were to make the rounds of all the laboratories, including the chemical labs and the animal labs. One afternoon when she assumed watch, a surgeon was waiting to give his report. He told her he had just done surgery on a baboon. Her orders were to make rounds on that baboon every hour and to feed him a little banana with long forceps. She was also instructed to use a big asepto syringe with a wide hose at the end to squirt water into his mouth. She wasn't to touch the baboon.

Every hour she faithfully made her rounds, and every hour he was sitting up in a wooden chair with his legs and arms shackled to the chair. At about 1 A.M., Miller tried to feed the baboon, but he wouldn't open his mouth. His big eyes stared straight ahead. She kept poking the banana at him, but he didn't flinch.

"I stood there and looked at him," she said. "There was no way I was going to listen with a stethoscope. I thought the baboon was dead."

She got the corpsman, and they went back downstairs to the baboon.

"Why don't you listen with stethoscope?" the corpsman asked.

"No, I don't want to touch him," Miller said. "I don't want him to come to, break out of his restraints, and take a leap at us."

Miller felt terrible. The doctor was going to think, "This Navy nurse can't even take care of a baboon."

She called the doctor and he came right over. "He's gone," the doctor said.

"I'm awfully sorry," Miller said. "I thought he was getting stiff."

"I'm not surprised," the doctor said. "We didn't expect him to live as long as you've kept him alive."

Miller wishes she had known that ahead of time. Maybe she wouldn't have worried so much. Throughout the years, Miller has been teased as the only one in the Nurse Corps who took care of a baboon and couldn't keep him alive.

After one year at the research institute, Duerk transferred Miller to the Health Sciences Education and Training Command (HSETC). For four years Miller served in developing and preparing a standardized Nurse Corps Orientation Program with 16mm films and videotapes. While working for HSETC from 1973 to 1976, Miller was promoted to commander.

Finally, Miller finished her career as a commander at the medical center at the Naval Submarine Base in Groton, Connecticut, where she worked from 1976 to 1982.

In her twenty-year career, Miller never experienced military sexual trauma. She traveled a lot to medical conferences where the majority of people were men, and she traveled cross-country by herself once. "I always had a book, and to this day I carry a book when I go someplace because I don't want to be bothered," she said. She'd order a meal and sit down with her face in the book until her meal arrived. "Oftentimes I had drinks put in front of me," she said.

"Where did that come from?" she'd ask.

"The gentleman over there."

"Take it away. I don't want it," she'd tell the waiter. "You can bet I wasn't looking to see who it was."

When you're independent, you have to make your own way. Miller didn't have brothers or sisters. Her mother and father brought her up to take care of herself. "I used to say to people, 'It takes two to tango.' If you go into a room looking all around, someone will be coming over," she said. "I didn't look at anybody. In a city. By yourself. You have to take care of yourself."

As to surviving the emotional toll of nursing wounded and mutilated patients over the years, Miller said it's simply part of her work. "You get busy," she said. "You didn't have time to think of yourself."

It's true she had time to think when she got home, but even then she stayed busy. She took out a lot of her frustration on the tennis court. She also rode her bike often in Japan and at home. If she had a day off in Japan, she hit the road, sightseeing or taking in a bath and massage. She'd go back to work a new person.

She has collected stamps since she was a child and loves to read, listen to classical music, and volunteer at her church. She volunteered in the Retired Activities Office (RAO) at the U.S. Naval Submarine Base in Groton for twenty years.

She doesn't have time for regrets. "I could sit here and look out the window and feel sorry for myself," she said. "But I have too much to do. There's so much to do in life."

Epilogue

LIFE IS TOUGH FOR VETERANS, ESPECIALLY THOSE WHO HAVE GONE to war or been sexually assaulted. But now more than ever, these veterans are facing their trauma head on, with the help of family, friends, and professionals. As they seek help, the question arises: What do women need from the military, the VA, family, and friends. They have much to deal with, much to heal from. How can we help?

Above all, while still serving in the military, women need to feel safe in their work environment and know they are taken seriously. There has been a fear among women who have been abused, assaulted, or harassed that nothing will change–that victims of military sexual trauma will continue not to report for fear of harassment, retaliation, and ostracism–that repeat offenders will find the military a perfect camouflage for their criminal behavior–that women who report military sexual trauma will continue to find their complaints career-ending.

Women, who make up 15 percent (and rising) of the military, are in the military to stay. The military needs to do a better job taking care of them. One way it can do this is to continue to support women (and men) reporting their military sexual trauma outside the chain of command. Zero tolerance must mean *zero tolerance*. This applies to all levels of command. Let military law enforcement, judge advocates, and area defense councils do exactly what they were set up to do, adjudicate crimes under the Constitution by using the rules promulgated by the Uniform Code of Military Justice. And if the military judicial system isn't working, then let the civilian judicial system handle these matters.

Everyone has to start seeing women as veterans, including the medical staff that treats them. Chelsea, a veteran, went to a military hospital when she was experiencing trauma related to her time in Iraq. She saw a corpsman, an E6, in sick call. She reported that she couldn't fall asleep, and when she did, she had a hard time staying asleep. She was experiencing anxiety and stress at night. She needed something to help her sleep. The conversation went something like this:

"Did you deploy?" he asked her.

"Yes."

"Were you in combat?"

"Kind of."

"Yes or no?"

"I was in dangerous areas," Chelsea responded. "I was part of a medical team on a base."

"Did you pull out your gun and shoot anyone, or did someone shoot you?"

"No."

"Then you weren't in combat," he said. "And if you didn't shoot anyone, you have no grounds for PTSD."

We need quality counselors who are knowledgeable about veterans—women veterans in particular—and the trauma they experience. In the Diagnostic and Statistical Manual of Mental Disorders (DSM), the description of PTSD is five pages long. There are eight diagnostic criteria for adults. For example, symptoms of PTSD can include recurrent distressing memories and/or dreams of the traumatic event, as well as flashbacks in which the individual feels as if the trauma was happening again. Chelsea had these symptoms and others from her work with mass casualties, but PTSD was ruled out because she hadn't shot anyone in combat. Moreover, early studies have shown that PTSD presents itself differently in women and men. For instance, women are more likely to show avoidance; men are more likely to be irritable and impulsive. Women are more likely to have mood and anxiety disorders; men are more likely to abuse drugs and alcohol. We need more research on women and PTSD.

I asked some female veterans what civilians can do to help them get on track. The answer is surprisingly simple. Be a witness—someone who will listen to veterans and celebrate their joys, someone who calls and says, "What can I do for you?" Be the person who has earned the right, the *trust*, to hear a veteran's story. Veterans want civilians to get to know them beyond their service. "We have first names too, and once you get to know them, many of us will share our stories with you," said veteran Kellie Noble Sharpe. "Just listen." Veteran Kathy Champion suggests that a civilian find one veteran who needs help and stick with that individual for two years, through good times and bad, and help her find footing to move forward in her community.

Some veterans would like to see something similar to AA meetings for veterans, a place where they can meet and socialize with other veterans outside the official channels of the VA. Veterans can share experiences with others who understand them. "I miss being surrounded by others," said veteran Denise Malloy, who was surrounded by soldiers day and night for years while she served in the military, a professional and social network that disappeared when she left. Her family and friends wanted to help, but it was difficult for them and her. "I don't want family and friends to know everything," Malloy said. "I want to protect them, and to not try to explain the unexplainable choices that were made by me or made for me." Along these lines, civilians can advocate for veterans' community centers, like neighborhood senior centers, places for veterans to hang out, take a class, play cards or shoot pool, attend activities and go on trips, and find out about benefits and resources.

The bottom line is that female veterans want to be known beyond their injuries and their Purple Hearts. They want to be known for their work ethic and their dedication. They want to be known for *who they are now.* These women are proud of their service and want to help others, but they don't want to live in the shadow of their service. "Almost every time I meet someone new–beyond even asking what my name is–they immediately want to know what happened to me," said veteran Amber Fifer, who was wounded in combat. "It makes me feel frustrated and isolated. I imagine other veterans feel the same way. If more people would see us for what we have to offer now, veterans would feel empowered to continue making progress and not feel overpowered by their past."

One of the issues that veterans have had to tackle over the years is medication for their mental problems. How much is too much? Women veterans overwhelmingly agree that healthcare providers, in and out of the military, are too quick to medicate. A Vietnam War veteran said she believes there is a tendency to medicate prior to sufficient investigation by a doctor, "partly because the doctors are swamped and partly because it is easier to medicate than to listen, *really* listen, to what is happening with someone." These veterans don't dismiss the short-term value of medication, but the long-term value is suspect. At what point is the medication doing more harm than good? What are the effects over a period of years? Can it make symptoms worse? Veteran Tegan Griffith said she challenges her doctors to find a way to help her without medicating her. Others have been frustrated by doctors who resist alternatives to medication or are reluctant to change prescriptions or dosages. Veteran Michelle Burns experienced thyroid problems from her antidepressant medication, and instead of adjusting the antidepressant, the VA put her on thyroid medication. "If I balk," she said, "I get threatened with noncompliance going into my file. I'm afraid of losing benefits. I reduced my meds on my own and stopped on altogether. I just don't tell the VA."

Women say the VA can do better in other ways as well. They could benefit from drop-in daycare for veterans with children or children-friendly waiting areas. They would also like separate waiting areas for women in the mental health clinic who are military sexual trauma survivors. Evening and Saturday appointments would be helpful for those with jobs. And assigning permanent providers in the specialty clinics, such as endocrinology, would provide continuity of care. Many veterans think, erroneously, that they are not eligible for VA care because of the nature of their discharge or their income level, or they see the VA as a "welfare system," with all its negative connotations. The VA needs to help veterans understand that VA care is an *earned* benefit, part of the benefits package that comes with employment in the military.

Healing a nation of warriors is everyone's responsibility. These are our warriors. These are our daughters, our sisters, our moms, our friends. May all veterans find the healing they need and deserve.